Cover by Roxanne Mei Lum

With ecclesiastical approval

ISBN 0-89870-371-9
Library of Congress catalogue number 91-71630
Printed in the United States of America

Dedicated
in Loving and Abiding Memory
to my parents

Michael J. Wrenn (+ April 20, 1989)
Elizabeth McBreen Wrenn (+ July 6, 1989)

Contents

Foreword

Since the days when the apostles turned to the Lord and asked him to teach them to pray, believers have been seeking to deepen their faith by piercing the mystery of God himself and the awesome gift of his Son Jesus who brought us redemption. This quest has both spiritual and academic dimensions, reflecting both the cognitive and affective dimensions of the human person. As our faith goes beyond mere feelings and utilizes God's gift of intellect to understand his often mysterious ways, the Church proclaims the love of God in the context of theological understandings which are both spiritually nourishing and academically challenging. Seen in hindsight, it seems as if one of the first tasks of the early Church was to provide her members with a coherent body of doctrine which could be easily understood and serve as an articulation of the common faith which they had received. From the Council of Jerusalem to our present day, the leaders of the Church have gathered to discuss, debate, and discern the core questions of our faith. The documents which result from these inspired discussions are themselves indications that Christ's promise never to abandon his Church is continually fulfilled through the gift of the teaching office of the bishops.

Rather than being a restrictive task, this vital role of teacher is a privileged way in which the bishops challenge and enable the faithful to grow in their faith by deepening their understanding of the truths which the Church has taught for centuries. All too often our culture views guidance as limitation, and thus deprives our contemporaries of the unique and rich legacy handed on to us by our forebears in the Church.

Recognizing this unfortunate misapprehension, the Second Vatican Council, itself taking place at a time of remarkable social and religious upheaval, charged the successors of the apostles with the task of providing the faithful with a clear and accurate summation of the teachings of the Church which the Council reaffirms in the sixteen documents which are the fruit of countless hours of labor.

A quarter century has quickly passed since the momentous closing days of the Council; years filled with controversy, misunderstanding, and some well-intended but misguided attempts to bring the conciliar teachings to the everyday lives of Catholics. In the midst of it all, steadfast faith and enduring traditions have sustained the Church throughout the many controversies which have racked her history. With the publication of the new *Catechism for the Universal Church,* the Church will receive yet another grace-filled gift; a reminder of Pentecost and an invitation to live the timeless truths of the gospel in our own age.

Each time I have the privilege of climbing the steps of the pulpit of Saint Patrick's Cathedral, I am humbled and inspired by what may only be called a real hunger on the part of the faithful gathered to learn more about the faith which we profess. Perhaps it is a result of too many years of ambivalence and equivocation. Definitely it is the fruit of the Holy Spirit, prodding all of us from bishop to layman to examine the doctrines of the Church and be renewed by their ever vibrant truths.

The proposed publication of the *Catechism for the Universal Church* has been met with applause by some, disdain by others. Monsignor Wrenn's volume is a fine preparation for all of us to receive the fruits of the theological expertise and precision in the catechism. In reading this book and awaiting the catechism with hopeful expectation, we are helped to recognize the opportunity to come to a new understanding of the truths which God has entrusted to his Church.

+ John Cardinal O'Connor
Archbishop of New York
Pentecost Sunday, 1991

Introduction

The Catechism for the Universal Church commissioned by the 1985 Synod of Bishops has been underway since 1985, twenty years after the end of the Second Vatican Council. This Catechism has already attracted some major attention and has even stirred up some lively controversy; this controversy was particularly marked on the occasion of the appearance of the first draft or "provisional text" of the Catechism in 1990, twenty-five years after the end of the Council. The Catechism now looks to be a reality in 1992, or shortly thereafter, and both friends and foes of the project agree at least on this: this Catechism may be the most important single document issued by the Church since the Second Vatican Council.

It may also prove to be one of the longest-lived of all the documents issuing from the Council or of the present era generally. The Catechism of the Council of Trent served pastors as a basic guide to the teaching of the Catholic faith for four hundred years, from 1566 to 1966. The Catechism for the Universal Church may end up being in service for an equally long period. Thus it is surely a document of the highest importance.

The process of preparing this Catechism has brought back to center stage the issue of catechesis, or the teaching of the faith. To too many people catechesis has often been thought to be a secondary issue with little excitement attached to it. This should not be the case, since handing on the faith that she has from Christ through the apostles and their successors, the bishops, is in many respects the most fundamental and enduring of the Church's missions. The Catholic faith lives only to the degree that the Church acting *in loco Christi* manages successfully to transmit that faith. How has that task been accomplished over the past quarter century since the Council?

It is time to take stock. It is time to attempt to understand what has been happening in religious education in the postconciliar years. It is time to try to understand better the reasons why a Catechism for the Universal Church came to be thought necessary as well as the context and environment into which this Catechism will be coming.

The present study aims to present catechesis, or religious education, in the context of the situation in the Church since Vatican II. It is well known that all has not been completely tranquil with respect to this subject during that particular period. It is the hope of many, in fact, that the promulgation of the new Catechism for the Universal Church will be precisely the thing that will provide a remedy for the many perceived problems that have beset religious education in the postconciliar years. Others seem not nearly so favorable about the prospect of a Churchwide Catechism issued in Rome; now that this prospect is virtually certain, it is of great interest and significance how the latter are already beginning to react even before the official promulgation of the final and definitive version of the Catechism for the Universal Church.

This is not a systematic treatment of religious education in the postconciliar years. Rather, it is an interpretative essay. It covers the highlights and provides examples only to illustrate the points being made. Many other things could be said about religious education, no doubt, but what is said here can confidently be asserted to be of major importance for the Church and the faith and the future. I have been occupied with questions of religious education for a major portion of my priestly life; yet much of what is brought out in these pages was a surprise even to me once I decided to try to delve more deeply into what has been going on in religious education in the years under study here: a Catechism for the Universal Church *is* necessary, indeed imperative.

One other point: this is a book for the general reader, the average Catholic interested in how the faith is to be taught. The aim is not to go too deeply into technicalities. For example, the terms "catechesis" and "religious education" will be used synonymously here, as they are in popular speech—and they refer to the ecclesial task of handing on the Church's faith in its authenticity and integrity. No other task is worthy of the catechist or religion teacher; no other task is more vital, either.

Chapter I

A Draft Catechism for the Universal Church and How It Was Created

1.

Some of the press stories that appeared in January 1990 resembled the kind of stories with which the Catholic public first became acquainted in the late nineteen-sixties: Catholic theologians and scholars were publicly confronting the Church. "In the first public critique of a new 'universal catechism' for the Roman Catholic Church", one of these press stories ran, "a group of Catholic scholars said yesterday the document's approach would stir confusion and division in the American Church. . . . [The Catechism] fails to distinguish between core Catholic beliefs and less essential ones, the scholars said at a press conference."[1]

Thus, what appeared to be an attempt by the Catholic Church to issue a foundational document setting forth her basic beliefs was, according to these Catholic scholars "at a press conference", itself alleged to be the possible cause of "confusion and division". The implications apparently were that Catholics today are already very clear about what they are supposed to believe; that official documents issued by the Church spelling it out in so many words could only muddle things up; and that Catholic theologians and scholars are not only competent to decide which Catholic beliefs are "core" and which are "less essential"—if necessary to decide this even against the official pronouncements of the Church—but are also the logical and natural protectors of the Catholic faithful from their bishops and, especially, from the Holy See in Rome.

[1] *Washington Times*, January 29, 1990.

For what was in question was indeed another teaching document from Rome, a document that the news story quoted above correctly identified as a "Catechism for the Universal Church" (not a "universal catechism", as the same news story otherwise kept referring to the document).

The Catechism all the fuss was about was a 434-page draft that had been sent out barely two months earlier to all of the world's some 3,000 Catholic bishops for comment. A covering letter dated November 3, 1989, was addressed to each recipient bishop; this letter was written on the stationery of something called "the Secretariat of the Commission for the Catechism for the Universal Church" and was signed by Cardinal Joseph Ratzinger, prefect of the Roman Congregation for the Doctrine of the Faith, but also head of this Commission. In his letter to each Catholic bishop, Cardinal Ratzinger said:

> As you know, the Holy Father wishes that the whole Catholic episcopate be consulted on this draft of the Catechism in order to prepare a magisterial text which will serve as a "point of reference" for National and Diocesan Catechisms. I would be grateful if you could send your observations, suggestions, and the proposals you deem opportune as to the entire draft of the Catechism herewith enclosed to the Secretariat of the Commission for the Catechism by the end of May, 1990.[2]

In other words, what was going on here was a consultation between a special Commission of bishops preparing a Catechism and the Catholic episcopate the world over. Far from handing down something from on high, as Rome is so often accused of doing, Cardinal Ratzinger was carefully soliciting "observations, suggestions, and . . . proposals" from bishops everywhere, and this at the specific request of Pope John Paul II. A "magisterial text", that is, an official teaching document issuing from the Church's magisterium, or teaching authority, was, to be sure, the intended result of this whole consultation process. Even then, however,

[2] Covering Letter accompanying the revised text of the draft Catechism for the Universal Church, Libreria Editrice Vaticana, Vatican City, 1989.

according to the Cardinal's express words, the resulting Catechism would not be something uniformly and monolithically imposed upon the whole Church but would be what Cardinal Ratzinger called a "point of reference" for national and diocesan catechisms. "Point of reference" appeared to mean something that could be referred to in case of uncertainty or dispute—hardly an instrument of arbitrary despotism!

How did such a careful and seemingly routine consultation between Rome and the worldwide Catholic episcopate on a subject normally so unnewsworthy as a "Catechism" ever give rise to sensational news stories about sowing "confusion and division" in the Church? And to public confrontation between Catholic scholars and theologians and official Church authority?

Actually, the new draft Catechism for the Universal Church sent out from Rome had quite a long and interesting history, many aspects of which will be looked at in these pages. Its proximate (though not its remote) origin was to be found in the 1985 extraordinary session of the Synod of Bishops assembled by Pope John Paul II to commemorate the twentieth anniversary of the Second Vatican Council of 1962–65. As will be seen, both the Commission for the Catechism for the Universal Church headed by Cardinal Ratzinger, as well as another (sub)commission of writers doing the actual drafting work, was entirely composed of bishops. When completed the Catechism will also be addressed primarily to bishops, since they will be primarily responsible for the national and diocesan catechisms for which the worldwide Catechism will be a "point of reference".

According to the faith of the Church, the bishops are the legitimate successors of the apostles of Jesus. Who, then, other than bishops, would most properly be engaged in preparing a Catechism for the Universal Church? The bishops in union with the Pope will be responsible for promulgating and implementing the Catechism when the time comes, just as certain ones of them have been responsible for assisting in its preparation. Thus, it was not at all unreasonable that those responsible for the Catechism, namely, the Pope and the bishops, acting under a mandate from the Synod of Bishops, might have wanted and needed to keep the process of its composition and completion in their own hands; nothing could have been more reasonable, in fact. And so it was actually the case that the worldwide consultation mentioned here was supposed to have been a confidential process, conducted among the bishops themselves. The provisional text of the Catechism sent out to all the bishops was plainly marked *"sub secreto"*. The news story quoted above referred to this fact when it spoke of a "confidential review" of the document. The text was not released to third parties, either by the Holy See or by the American bishops' conference.

This did not mean that the bishops could not show it to their own theologians or advisors or be helped by the latter. It did mean, though, that decisions about and control of the composition process was to remain directly in the hands of bishops and not be given over, for example, to a group of "Catholic scholars" so that the latter could provide a "public critique" of it. If wider consultation had been desired, it could easily have been requested, as it has been requested in the case of some other Church documents. In going directly to the press with their public critique, these scholars were clearly treading on somebody else's ground and usurping a function that did not belong to them.

How did it come about that a group of Catholic scholars was suddenly offering a public critique of a *sub secreto* Church document at a press conference? It came about because the Catholic scholars in question did not like or did not agree with what they found in the draft, however they may have come into possession of copies of it; and hence they evidently wanted to use whatever public means available to them to head off and discredit the document before it even had a chance to be completed and promulgated.

The press and media are generally avid, of course, to report on disputes, disagreements, and confrontations within the Catholic Church, these things being considered more newsworthy than the Church's humdrum everyday work of reconciling and sanctifying sinners and leading them to salvation. It was therefore not surprising that the press conference in question produced a number of stories; another juicy disagreement in the Church was at issue, after all. Thus it was that, probably for most Catholics, the first public news that a new Catechism was even being prepared came in a story featuring the opposition to it on the part of those Catholic scholars who were criticizing it. The process is familiar to all those who remember how, back in 1968, Pope Paul VI's famous encyclical *Humanae Vitae* upholding the Church's traditional teaching against contraception was first reported to the public in stories that were mainly about the opposition to the encyclical of the theologians who were dissenting from it.

In fact, it proved that the gathering of Catholic scholars to criticize the new Catechism was something more than just a press conference. It was a fullblown, scholarly "symposium", consisting of some fifteen papers delivered by various experts on various aspects of the Catechism. Sponsored by the Woodstock Theological Center at Georgetown University in Washington, D.C., it took place only a little more than a month after copies of the document being criticized could even have been received by the bishops of the United States to whom it had been addressed. The symposium organizers and participants had clearly had to move with lightning speed to have managed to put the thing on at all—unless they were lying in wait for the Catechism all along and had access to bootlegged copies of it.

The *longueurs* usually encountered in book publishing today also seem to have been cut considerably short in the case of this project. For by November 1990 a full-fledged book with the title *The Universal Catechism Reader* had found its way into print; it consisted of the fifteen symposium papers, suitably revised, and edited by Father Thomas J. Reese, S.J., a senior fellow at the Woodstock Center.[3] In celebration of this book's appearance, yet another public "Woodstock Forum", featuring Father Reese

[3] Thomas J. Reese, S.J., ed., *The Universal Catechism Reader: Reflections and Responses* (San Francisco: Harper Row, 1990).

and three of his coauthors, was held before an appreciative audience at Georgetown University on November 28, 1990. Anyone who may have thought the prospect of this Roman Catechism was not a timely and newsworthy subject was clearly mistaken. There turned out to be plenty of interest in the subject!

How there could ever be a valid "reader" on the subject of a document that had not yet been completed, much less promulgated, though, is difficult for an uninitiated observer to credit. The purpose of such a reader seems clearly not to have been in this case to help in the understanding and appreciation of the document it purported to treat. Indeed the reader in question seems to be more about what a group of self-appointed theologians and experts think ought to be in a Church Catechism than about what the official teachers in the Church were trying to put into it. There seems to have been more than just a suggestion in the choice of a title that the theologians and experts were properly the ones to say what ought to be in the document they erroneously persist in calling the "Universal Catechism". No reader opening up *The Universal Catechism Reader,* by the way, will be disabused of this initial impression of asserted competence and omniscience.

Meanwhile, some of the symposium papers that became book chapters had already achieved wide notoriety and diffusion by means of periodical publication. *America* magazine's issue of March 3, 1990, and *Commonweal* magazine's issue of March 9, 1990, published a number of the papers with appropriate fanfare. According to the book's editor, Father Reese, copies of these articles were also sent to all the American bishops and to episcopal conferences around the world. There was clearly no hesitation on the part of the symposium participants and authors about the legitimacy of their enterprise. A measure of quiet pride even shows through in Father Reese's enumeration of all the press coverage garnered by the symposium and the subsequent publication of papers from it.[4] That few or none of these press stories critical of the Catholic Church, her leadership, and her procedures can really have advanced

[4] Ibid., p. 219, n. 10.

the cause of the saving faith that the Church represents seems not to have been a consideration.

After all, the Middle Ages are long past; this is America; this is the twentieth century, almost the twenty-first! If the Pope and the bishops ever really imagined that they could succeed in producing a Catechism for the Church on their own terms, then they surely richly deserved the sharp comeuppance administered to them by the Woodstock Theological Center, Georgetown University, *America* and *Commonweal* magazines, and so on. No more than "the best and the brightest" of a decade or so ago in America could attempt to conduct a war without being undermined by the publication of the Pentagon Papers, can churchmen or any other public figures today expect to do anything whatsoever *sub secreto*. America is a democracy, after all; the First Amendment reigns; it is all going to become public regardless, and the Pope and the bishops might as well get used to it.

However, those who actually believe Vatican II's teaching that "the Catholic Church is by the will of Christ the teacher of truth"—a "sacred and certain teaching", the Council specified[5] —may wonder whether the extended media event engineered so successfully by Father Reese and his colleagues has really delivered the last word on the subject of the Catechism for the Universal Church or even its "provisional text". What they have attempted, rather, is a "pre-emptive strike" on the document (if another Pentagon example may figuratively serve here): by ambushing both the process and the product of the Church's universal catechetical enterprise as it has manifested itself to date, they evidently hoped to compromise and discredit the final and definitive Catechism for the Universal Church before it ever had a chance to be brought out in any final and definitive form. By their own abundant testimony, not to speak of "overkill", the draft that was produced was not to their liking; nor was the process to their liking, either: Bishops actually overseeing and writing their own document? Unheard of! What next? In the view of those who

[5] Vatican Council II, *Dignitatis Humanae*, no. 14.

think in this fashion it was evident that a quite exceptional effort was called for to cast a pall over the whole project before it went any farther (they probably understood that they could never succeed in derailing the project entirely). Thus, a quite exceptional effort was made.

These detractors themselves signal the importance of the document they are trying so hard to neutralize: When has a Church document ever attracted so much attention even before being published? There is evidently more here than meets the eye. What is this Catechism for the Universal Church, who wanted it, why is it being prepared, why are some "Catholic scholars" apparently so adamantly if not violently opposed to it, and how is it all going to come out?

What does seem pretty clear at this point is that while the Pope and the bishops may be following a definite and easily understood agenda in producing a Catechism for the Universal Church, at least a faction of Catholic scholars appears to have another and different agenda entirely, an agenda that these scholars appear determined to pursue regardless of what the leaders of their Church may have wished or may wish. In pursuing their agenda, moreover, these scholars are only too likely to continue to enjoy a free ride courtesy of the media; the media understand very well that there is another agenda at work here; they understand and favor it because they know that the successful pursuit of this agenda will impair the effectiveness of the Catholic Church in carrying out the true mission she has from Christ. It is unfortunate that the Catholic faithful, and sometimes even their bishops, do not always appear to understand the effects of this other agenda at work as well as the mass media do.

2.

The idea of developing a Catechism for the Universal Church originated as one of the suggestions forwarded to the Holy Father as a result of an extraordinary session of the Synod of Bishops held in the fall of 1985. Today people are getting used to reading about successive sessions of the Synod of Bishops held in Rome, but these synodal meetings of representatives of the Catholic Church's world episcopate with the successor of Peter are actually a relatively recent, postconciliar phenomenon. Vatican Council II decreed:

> Bishops chosen from different parts of the world in a manner and according to a system determined or to be determined by the Roman Pontiff will render to the Supreme Pastor a more effective auxiliary service in a council which shall be known by the special name of Synod of Bishops. This council, as it will be representative of the whole Catholic episcopate, will bear testimony to the participation of all the bishops in hierarchical communion in the care of the universal Church.[6]

By an Apostolic Letter, *Apostolica Sollicitudo,* of September 15, 1965, Pope Paul VI officially established the Synod of Bishops. The successive sessions of this permanent Synod feature a representative selection of bishops from around the world, either elected by their own bishops' conferences or appointed by the Holy Father; these representative bishops meet every few years in Rome to consider topical questions facing the Church and to advise the Holy Father accordingly. There are both "ordinary" and "extraordinary" synodal sessions.

As a result of these successive sessions since 1967 of the Synod of Bishops, a new type of teaching document, the "apostolic exhortation", has emerged in the Church. This has become a type of teaching document prepared and promulgated by the pope with the assistance of the Roman Curia, but one based upon considerable, and sometimes even comprehensive, input from the working sessions of the Synod. For centuries the popes have utilized "encyclicals" as one of their most common teaching vehicles, and, of course, they have not ceased to issue encyclicals today, just as, prior to the era of the Synod, they also issued apostolic exhortations from time to time. Following upon the various sessions of the Synod, however, both Pope Paul VI and Pope John

[6] Vatican Council II, *Christus Dominus,* no. 5.

Paul II have issued postsynodal apostolic exhortations utilizing the detailed deliberations and recommendations of the Synod sessions to excellent advantage. Thus in 1975, Pope Paul VI issued *Evangelii Nuntiandi* on the subject of evangelization in the modern world based on the 1974 ordinary Synod session. The 1977 ordinary Synod session was on catechesis, or the teaching of the faith, and as a result of it, Pope John Paul II issued in 1979 his apostolic exhortation *Catechesi Tradendae.* In view of its subject, this document, of course, is of special pertinence to the present study and will be noted and quoted rather frequently in these pages. Still another one of Pope John Paul II's apostolic exhortations pertinent to the present study, it turns out, is *Reconciliatio et Paenitentia,* issued in December 1984, following the labors of the 1983 Synod session on the subject of reconciliation and penance.

Yet other apostolic exhortations have proved significant (though less relevant to the present study): *Familiaris Consortio* issued in 1981 on the family followed the 1980 ordinary synodal session on that subject; and *Christifideles Laici* issued in 1988 followed the 1987 ordinary synodal session on the subject of the laity. No doubt the 1990 session on the priesthood will turn out to have inspired an equally important teaching document on that most vital of topics when the Pope issues it.

In accordance with Vatican II's original idea of the value of a permanent Synod of Bishops, one would have expected these postsynodal apostolic exhortations to enjoy an enhanced value, and even authority, as teaching documents, arising as they do out of an active collaboration between the pope and the bishops. Yet this does not seem to be the case; these postsynodal apostolic exhortations do not appear to constitute any greater deterrent to today's "pick-and-choose Catholicism" than papal encyclicals do these days. The whole idea of having a Synod was supposed to have been one of Vatican II's more liberal enactments; the actual results of the synodal process, however, have turned out to be regarded, in the event, deeply disappointing in certain quarters of the Church.

The 1985 Synod session was an extraordinary session. It was

convoked by Pope John Paul II in order to commemorate the Second Vatican Council twenty years after the close of that event. Vatican II, the Holy Father declared in convoking this extraordinary Synod session, was "a fundamental event in the life of the contemporary Church", and, as the Pope believed, it was

> necessary to refresh ourselves incessantly at that fountain . . . to relive in some fashion that extraordinary atmosphere of ecclesial communion which marked the ecumenical council through reciprocal sharing in the sufferings and joys, the struggles and hopes, experienced by the Body of Christ in various parts of the world; to exchange and deepen experiences and information on the application of the council, both at the universal and local level of the Church; and to promote further deepening and constant penetration by the Second Vatican Council into the life of the Church and also in the light of fresh demands as well.[7]

The 1985 Synod did not disappoint. It attracted an unusual amount of attention at the time. Precisely because it was called to commemorate the much-misunderstood event that was Vatican II and to "deepen", in the Pope's words, the proper "application" of that Council, many observers felt that this special Synod was somehow intended by the Pope to call a halt to or even to "roll back" the reforms of Vatican II and somehow move the Church back to a "preconciliar" stance. This kind of interpretation meant, of course, that one misunderstood what an ecumenical council is in general and what Vatican II was in particular. Certainly many legitimate changes in Church practice (though not in Church belief) were decreed during and after Vatican II. Not all of the changes that came about after the Council were decreed by it, however; it is crucially important to understand this. Honest mistakes were made in implementing Vatican II; some wrong turns were taken, of which the popes have been well aware; nor have the popes been anything but quite candid in adopting the

[7] Pope John Paul II, Address to the Curia, "Implementing the 1985 Synod", in *Origins,* NC Documentary Service, August 14, 1986.

stance that corrective action has been needed in the case of some of the Vatican II changes. Then, in addition to the changes actually desired by the Council, there have been others introduced by individuals and groups on their own; with regard to these latter, the stance of the popes has been that corrective action has been needed in properly implementing the Council. The normal responsibilities of leadership in any institution would have dictated policies and actions very close to those the popes have actually followed in the wake of Vatican II.

Meanwhile, the sixteen documents issued by the Council, followed by many other implementing documents stemming from the conciliar enactments, have long since become fixed and definitive parts of the Church's permanent patrimony and tradition. There is simply no way that the Council, understood in this fashion, *could* ever have been "rolled back" or somehow repudiated by the Synod; the very notion of imagining the Pope or Synod ever even being able to do such a thing was to see the Council in grossly politicized terms—that is, in a wholly distorted way considering what Church councils really are.

Nevertheless, many observers, especially those of a liberal or progressive bent, persisted in seeing the 1985 Synod as a largely reactionary phenomenon. "The Synod is designed to permit the world's bishops to advise the pope on matters of common interest", one such observer wrote. "But Pope John Paul . . . turned previous Synods into rallies for his own policies. So this extraordinary Synod will be invited to confirm not so much Vatican II as the pope's analysis of what the Church needs today. It is now clear what that is, and Cardinal Joseph Ratzinger, chief Vatican ideologue, has pronounced the key word: restoration."[8]

Cardinal Ratzinger, in particular, was seen as the bogeyman or bugbear of the 1985 Synod, a fact pertinent to the present study, as will be seen: no proposal (such as the proposal for a Catechism for the Universal Church) issuing from such a "reactionary" Synod as the 1985 one could possibly be valid for those who interpret

[8] Peter Hebblethwaite, *National Catholic Reporter,* February 8, 1985.

Vatican II as having begun a process of transforming the Church into a "democratic" institution. From this point of view, Cardinal Ratzinger was almost inescapably the "heavy". The *New York Times Magazine,* for example, came out with a cover story on him under the title, "The Pope's Guardian of Orthodoxy". In some ways this article was genuinely admiring of the German cardinal's considerable and undeniable attainments; on the other hand, it also retailed such attacks on him as Hans Küng's characterization of his curial position as "self-righteousness, ahistoricism, and blindness . . . something one would not have thought possible in the light of the remarkable theological work which this man produced in the 60s."[9]

In reality, the tasks set forth by John Paul II for the 1985 Synod were, if anything, legitimated by this kind of exaggerated journalistic account of what was going on and what was at stake at the Synod. In this regard, the comments on this same Synod by a prelate who was himself considered to have been one of the most "liberal" of the bishops at Vatican II can be quoted most pertinently here. Cardinal Gerald Emmett Carter, archbishop of Toronto, wrote as follows in a pastoral letter of his in October 1985, one month before the Synod:

> Some have chosen to interpret this [Synod] project in a negative fashion, as if [the pope] were requesting a recantation of the council or at least a disavowal of some of its more positive and far-reaching orientations. For me it is a logical, nay an almost required, underlining of the most important ecclesial event of the twentieth century. Not to have undertaken a special commemoration would have appeared as at least a doubtful attitude. . . .

Cardinal Carter also believed some corrective action had become necessary:

> . . . Unfortunate exaggerations . . . have taken place within the Church itself: liturgical eccentricities, disregard of the magiste-

[9] Quoted in E. J. Dionne, Jr., "The Pope's Guardian of Orthodoxy", *New York Times Magazine,* November 24, 1985.

> rium and of authority, libertinism in the concept of the formation of conscience, the downgrading of the eucharist and the ministerial priesthood, a false irenicism, and a host of other manifestations of what is called "the spirit of the council" and which never in any way presided over the spirit of the real council and which would have been indignantly rejected by the unanimity of the fathers of the council had it ever been presented to them. . . .

The Toronto cardinal, a veteran of Vatican II, thought the 1985 Synod was exactly what was required to help remedy the situation he was describing. He wrote in this pastoral letter:

> What is important at this juncture is that the extraordinary Synod speak clearly to theologians, to catechists, and to all the faithful concerning the right of the magisterium to teach and to bind all of the Catholic faithful. If the false and exaggerated ideas of parallel magisterium, of individual judgment on theological matters, of free dissent in "sacred and certain" Church teaching are allowed to grow and proliferate, the very unity of the Church is in danger.[10]

" . . . The right of the magisterium to teach and bind all of the Catholic faithful. . . . " Here, indeed, was a thought to float at the Woodstock Theological Center. This was strong language, as it was a tall order for the Synod. Coming from a Vatican II "liberal" bishop, it was especially significant. The 1985 Synod managed it all quite creditably, however. The fact that a positive and amicable spirit reigned at the Synod was itself a plus; the journalists covering the event sat around waiting for the fireworks they had been writing about to explode and schism—or something—to break out. Nothing of the sort occurred, of course; no harsh anathemas or excommunications were voiced. A number of concrete suggestions for follow-up action were, however, voted by the Synod fathers, of which the ones most worthy of note were the ones singled out by the Holy Father in his closing address to this 1985

[10] Cardinal Gerald Emmett Carter, "Issues for the 1985 Extraordinary Synod", in *Origins,* NC Documentary Service, November 7, 1985.

extraordinary session of the Synod of Bishops. These important suggestions were, in the words of John Paul II:

> —The desire expressed to prepare a compendium or catechism of all Catholic doctrine to serve as a point of reference for catechisms or compendia on this theme in all the particular churches; this desire responds to a real need both of the universal Church and of the particular churches.
>
> —The deepening of the study of the nature of the episcopal conferences, which in our time offer a precious contribution to the life of the Church.
>
> —The publication, finally, of the Code of Canon Law for the Eastern-rite churches, according to the tradition of these churches and the norms of Vatican II.[11]

These, then, were the principal "suggestions" that came out of the 1985 Synod. Naturally, the one for "a compendium or catechism of all Catholic doctrine" is the one of interest to the present study. And the idea for this particular recommendation was presented at the Synod by an American prelate, Cardinal Bernard Law, archbishop of Boston, who strongly voiced the need for an authoritative compendium of irreducible Catholic doctrine in this age of the "global village" and the mass media in which national catechisms could no longer necessarily fulfill the need for a contemporary articulation of the Church's faith. Cardinal Law wanted a commission of cardinals to prepare a draft catechism that the Holy Father would then promulgate, after consultation with all the bishops of the world.[12] The basic idea caught on. By the end of the session, eight of the nine synodal language-working groups were calling for the same thing. It was one of those ideas whose time came quickly. The Final Report of the Synod expressed itself more concretely in recommending the new Catechism than the Holy Father did in accepting it, as quoted above. Hence it is worth quoting the Synod specifications in full:

[11] Pope John Paul II, "Closing Address to the Synod", in *Origins,* NC Documentary Service, December 19, 1985.

[12] *L'Osservatore Romano,* English ed., December 9, 1985.

> Very many have expressed the desire that a catechism or compendium of all Catholic doctrine regarding both faith and morals be composed, that it might be, as it were, a point of reference for the catechisms or compendiums that are prepared in the various regions. The presentation of doctrine must be biblical and liturgical. It must be sound doctrine suited to the present life of Christians.[13]

Particular note should be taken here of the fact that the proposed new Catechism was to be both "biblical and liturgical" in its presentation of doctrine and that it was to present "sound doctrine, suited to the present life of Christians". Taken in its total context, the Synod's recommendation for a Catechism bespoke a grave concern for the teaching of what was styled "sound doctrine". In the very same section of the Final Report where the Catechism was recommended, in fact, the Synod expressed a similar concern for the proper formation of priests, indicating that they were to be trained in the manner called for in Vatican II's Decree on the Training of Priests no. 16. In that cited paragraph, it is plainly stated that the theological subjects given to aspiring priests "should be taught in the light of faith under the guidance of the magisterium of the Church".[14] Given this context of overall concern for sound doctrine, it is not surprising that the Holy Father quickly picked up on these very same points.

A year later, reporting to the Roman Curia on the progress made in carrying out the recommendations of the Synod, Pope John Paul II specified that the very purpose of the new Catechism was nothing else but "to put an end to teaching or interpretations of the faith or morals which are not in accord with each other or with the universal magisterium".[15] This original purpose should not be lost sight of in evaluating the draft Catechism for the Universal Church that finally issued from Rome late

[13] "The Final Report of the 1985 Extraordinary Synod of Bishops", in *Origins,* NC Documentary Service, December 19, 1985.

[14] Vatican Council II, *Optatam Totius,* no. 16.

[15] John Paul II, "Implementing 1985 Synod".

in 1989, only to be attacked by the Woodstock group of scholars, *because,* as will be seen, it stated clearly Catholic doctrine without the theological nuances some appeal to today as the pretext for not stating Catholic doctrine clearly. What the Synod actually specified the Catechism for the Universal Church should be must also be taken into account in evaluating the final product when it appears.

Indeed it is worth stating here, especially in view of the discussion to follow, that a catechism, any catechism, is, by definition, concerned with Catholic *doctrine;* it is nothing else but a "compendium of doctrine". That a catechism embodies and sets forth established doctrine cannot intelligibly be a point of criticism of it; this would be like criticizing a church for being involved with worship or a school for being involved with education. Of course it is quite true that the Catholic faith is more, much more, than mere doctrine; a living faith is expressed in the Scriptures, in liturgy and worship, and in the living of the Christian life; it is not the mere spouting of doctrine. Nevertheless doctrine remains an indispensable foundation stone of authentic faith. And what a catechism is all about, any catechism, is this doctrinal foundation of the Catholic faith. Again: it *cannot* be a legitimate object of reproach of a catechism to say that it is "too" doctrinal and ignores other aspects of the faith; it necessarily assumes and takes for granted those other aspects of the faith; but it remains what it is.

Pope John Paul II moved quickly on the Synod's recommendation for a compendium of doctrine for the Church as a whole. On June 10, 1986, the Commission for the Catechism for the Universal Church was named, with Cardinal Ratzinger, almost inevitably, as its head; the two American prelates on the Commission were Cardinal William Baum, then prefect of the Congregation for Catholic Education, and Cardinal Bernard Law of Boston, who had initially suggested the undertaking. The original announcement of the naming of the Commission noted that it was expected to complete its work in time for the 1990 ordinary session of the Synod of Bishops and the twenty-fifth anniversary of the Second

Vatican Council.[16] This was not to be, as it turned out, even though Pope John Paul II had strongly expressed the same wish.[17] This is a point of importance to note since Church authorities were later sharply criticized for not allowing sufficient time for the world episcopate to comment on the draft that was produced and circulated, allegedly because they wanted to rush their text through without giving others time to study and properly react to it. However, the request to the bishops of the world to try to have their comments on the draft back by May 1990 was nothing more than a valiant attempt to hold to a schedule firmly laid down years before; it was unnecessary and unfair to try to read sinister motives into this original May deadline.

When Cardinal Ratzinger reported on the progress of the catechism project at the 1987 ordinary session of the Synod of Bishops, he was still quite optimistic that the final text would be completed in time for presentation to the 1990 ordinary session of the Synod. On that occasion he also reported that a Secretariat for the Catechism Commission had been formed, consisting primarily of support personnel from his own Congregation, as well as a (sub)commission of writers (styled an "editorial committee" in the provisional text itself); this editorial committee also consisted entirely of bishops. In addition, what Cardinal Ratzinger called a "college of consultors" was unveiled, consisting of about forty experts to be consulted. The editorial committee doing the actual

[16] *Origins,* NC Documentary Service, August 14, 1986. The complete membership of the Commission included: Cardinal Joseph Ratzinger, prefect of the Congregation for the Doctrine of the Faith; Cardinals William Baum and Antonio Innocenti, prefects of the Congregations for Catholic Education and the Clergy, respectively; Cardinal Jozef Tomko, prefect of the Congregation for the Evangelization of Peoples; Cardinal Simon Lourdusamy, prefect of the Congregation for Eastern Churches; Archbishop Jan Schotte, general secretary of the Synod of Bishops; Cardinal Bernard Law, archbishop of Boston; Archbishop Jerzy Stroba of Poznan, Poland; Greek Melkite Archbishop Neophytos Edelby of Aleppo, Syria; Indian Archbishop Henry Sebastian D'Souza of Calcutta, India; Coadjutor Archbishop Isidore de Souza of Cotonou, Benin, Africa; and Bishop Felipe Benitez Avalos of Villarrica, Paraguay.

[17] Ibid.

writing included an American bishop, Archbishop William Levada of Portland, Oregon. Also assigned to the editorial committee as an editing secretary was an Austrian priest, Father Christoph von Schönborn, O.P., of the University of Fribourg.[18] Among the Americans included among the forty expert consultors were Bishop Donald W. Wuerl of Pittsburgh and Father Francis Kelly of the National Catholic Education Association (NCEA).[19]

The main lines of the draft Catechism that would eventually emerge were already evident at the time Cardinal Ratzinger made his report to the 1987 Synod. In particular, Cardinal Ratzinger reported on the decision that this Catechism was to be "directed to those who have the task of composing and/or approving the national and/or diocesan catechisms. It is destined therefore especially for bishops, insofar as they are doctors of the faith: to them this Catechism is offered as an instrument for performing their prophetic office among the People of God, which is their own and which they cannot abdicate."[20]

The 434-page draft Catechism for the Universal Church, styled a "provisional text" on its cover page, was finally sent out for comment to all the Catholic bishops of the world in November 1989, with comments to be returned within what then seemed to be an ample six-month time period. This provisional Catechism

[18] Cardinal Joseph Ratzinger, "Toward a Universal Catechism or Compendium of Doctrine", in *Origins,* NC Documentary Service, November 5, 1987. The entire membership of the commission of writers included: Bishop José M. Estepa Llaurens, military ordinary for Spain; Bishop José Honoré, bishop of Tours, France; Bishop Alessandro Maggiolini, bishop of Carpi, Italy; Bishop Jorge Medina Estevez, apostolic administrator of Rancagua, Chile; Bishop David Konstant, bishop of Leeds, England; Archbishop William J. Levada, archbishop of Portland in Oregon; and Bishop Estanislao Esteban Karlich, archbishop of Parana, Argentina. Rev. Christoph von Schonborn, O.P., was named secretary. The composition of this editorial or drafting committee is interesting in view of the fact that the document was written in English, French, and Spanish, with translations into German and Italian; there is no "original" Latin version.

[19] *Origins,* CNS Documentary Service, March 8, 1990.

[20] Ratzinger, "Toward a Universal Catechism".

was the end result of years of thought and effort by all the various commissions, committees, and consultors, as well as the Catechism Secretariat staff. This product was quite clearly, as it was meant to be, a document of the bishops, by the bishops, and for the bishops in the first instance. Though ultimately intended to serve all the People of God, it was also intended to serve them through the instrumentality and mediation of their legitimate shepherds, the bishops, placed over all the People of God by the will of Christ.

As it turned out, the document proved to be quite familiar and traditional in its overall general format; but this was as it should be, according to all of the indications reviewed up to this point. In format the document is no doubt very close to what the final product will look like: it is divided into a Prologue and four main parts: the Apostles' Creed, the Sacraments, the Ten Commandments, and the Our Father. The Prologue examines what it means to say "I believe". The first, credal part corresponds to what the document also calls "the faith professed". The second part on the seven sacraments corresponds to what is called "the faith celebrated". The third part on the commandments covers the moral life and is styled "the faith lived". The Epilogue is called simply "the Our Father", after the foundational prayer given to the disciples by Jesus when they asked him to teach them to pray (cf. Lk 11:1).

Under all these various headings is set forth in considerable detail and with copious illustrative quotations the comprehensive content of "the Catholic faith that comes to us from the apostles" (First Eucharistic Prayer). This detailed and comprehensive statement of the faith is accompanied by a quite extraordinary collection of diverse quotations and citations from virtually every period of the Church's long and varied history, including especially the period of Vatican II and the postconciliar period, but also, heavily, New Testament and Patristic times. The document similarly draws from every possible source: Scripture, liturgy, prayers, sermons, catechisms, theological treatises, decisions of popes and councils—or, again, saints, popes, bishops, theologians, canonists, mystics, doctors of the Church. By almost any standard, the document is a remarkable production, especially for a draft. Considering the territory it covers and the fact that it was composed by a committee, the document also shows evidence—as was to be expected—of lacunae, certain exaggerations, overemphases (and some underemphases as well!), and more than a few other ragged edges. But then that was the whole point of a consultation with the world episcopate: there was never any claim that this provisional text was a finished product; indeed the contrary.

As indicated earlier, the aim of the present study is to look at the catechetical environment into which the new Catechism for the Universal Church will be coming when it is completed; it is therefore not a primary aim of this study to analyze the provisional text itself in depth. The present writer's thoughts, and suggestions on the text have been submitted through ecclesiastical channels, after they were requested by the Ordinary of the Archdiocese to which I belong. All in all, though, it is hard for anyone who has actually seen the text to understand why any group of Catholic scholars should think it to be their mission to try to bring the whole enterprise into disrepute before it could even be completed: the experience of the Church has been that her final definitive documents regularly demonstrate huge improvements on any drafts that have been made available; this is particularly true of documents whose authenticity will be guaranteed by the Holy See. The promise of the assistance of the Holy Spirit in a special way to the successor of Peter does not count for nothing here.

Besides, even the provisional text of this Catechism does not belong to its self-appointed critics; it belongs to the Pope and the bishops, the official teachers in the Church. Moreover, it contains nothing that is not already found in existing creeds, catechisms, papal and council documents, and so on, by which the Church already expresses her faith and by which Catholics are already bound. The credenda expected of Catholics by the Church are already both knowable and known, and this long before any Catechism for the Universal Church was ever dreamed of. This is not something the Polish Pope and Cardinal Ratzinger have made up on their own to "impose" on modern educated Catholics with nuanced theologies; it is a compendium of already existing—and known—doctrine.

Nevertheless a look at some of the objections of the Catholic scholars who have criticized the provisional text is going to be necessary, if only to try to determine who these people are and where they think they are coming from. First, however, it is important to review briefly the purposes that authoritative catechisms have served in the Church generally as well as why the Catechism for the Universal Church came to be thought necessary at all.

3.

In the early Church the Catholic faith was first preached and taught to adults converting to the new Way of Jesus. Candidates for baptism into the faith, or catechumens, as they were called, were given special systematic instruction in the faith, usually during Lent for baptism at Easter. This oral public instruction, which was also regularly given as part of the celebration of the Eucharist, was the oldest form of catechesis in the Church; it was originally given to adults and children indiscriminately, and all the evidence indicates, or, rather, the lack of any documentary evidence indicates, that it was generally left up to Christian parents and godparents to instruct their children in the truths of the faith. Thus initially, catechesis was not simply a process of teaching the faith to children, as it is too often thought to be today.

This same general pattern of oral preaching and teaching persisted for a very long period in the Church, from the earliest nonbiblical handbook on instruction in the faith, the *Didache,* or *Teaching of the Twelve Apostles,* as it was known, possibly dating from as early as 60 to 90 A.D. Instructional treatises became more numerous from the fourth century on and included such works as the *Catecheses* of Saint Cyril of Jerusalem, the *De Mysteriis* of Saint Ambrose of Milan, and the *Commentarius in Symbolum Apostolorum* of Rufinus of Aquileia. The same system persisted into the high medieval period, as a canon of the provincial Council of Beziers stipulated in 1246:

> . . . parish priests [must] see to it that they explain to the people on Sundays the articles of faith in simple and clear fashion so that no one may claim a veil of ignorance. . . . Children too from seven upwards, brought to church by their parents on Sundays and feasts, shall be instructed in the Catholic faith, and parents shall teach them *Mary's Salutation,* the *Our Father,* and the *Creed.*[21]

Any examination of the teaching of the faith in the early Church quickly reveals that there was always a doctrine or content to the faith, a "teaching", something definite that the Church transmitted or handed down. The idea that the faith lacks any definite content in particular and consists simply of the "Christian spirit" or something of the sort is an idea unknown to historic Christianity. As Professor J. N. D. Kelly of Oxford wrote in his authoritative *Early Christian Creeds:* "The early Church was from the start a believing, confessing, preaching Church. . . . It is impossible to overlook the emphasis on the transmission of authoritative doctrine which is found everywhere in the New Testament."[22]

This "authoritative doctrine" being transmitted, of course, was nothing else but the "good news" itself, the message of salvation in and through Jesus Christ working through his Church. The proclamation, or basic announcement, of this "good news" was expressed by the Greek word *kerygma,* a "proclamation"; the word was related to the Greek word *keryx,* meaning "herald". The apostles appointed and sent out by Jesus, like the successors they themselves appointed, the bishops of the Church, were thus nothing else but "heralds" of faith in and salvation through Jesus Christ.

[21] See especially Gerald S. Sloyan, "Religious Education: From Early Christianity to Medieval Times", in Michael Warren, ed., *Sourcebook for Modern Catechetics* (Winona, Minn.: St. Mary's Press, 1983), pp. 110–39.

[22] J. N. D. Kelly, *Early Christian Creeds,* 3d ed. (London: Longman, 1972), pp. 7–8.

One example of this basic apostolic *kerygma* is to be found in 1 Corinthians 15, where Saint Paul declared:

> Brothers, I want to remind you of the Gospel I preached to you, which you received and in which you stand firm. You are being saved by it at this very moment if you hold fast to it as I preached it to you. . . . I handed on to you first of all what I myself received, that Christ died for our sins in accordance with the Scriptures; that he was buried and, in accordance with the Scriptures, rose on the third day, that he was seen by Cephas, then by the Twelve. . . . After that he was seen by five hundred brothers at once. . . . Next he was seen by James; then by all the apostles. Last of all he was seen by me. . . . This is what we preach, and this is what you believed . . . (1 Cor 15:1–8, 11).

This is only one example of the kind of apostolical *kerygma* to be found in the New Testament; another example would be the *kerygma* of Saint Peter recorded in Acts 2:14–36. Such proclamations of the faith always possessed definite content or doctrine; this latter word, "doctrine", originates from Latin *docere,* "to teach", and means "that which is taught"; the believer in Jesus was expected and obliged to hear this "doctrine" and assent to it; it was part of having faith in Jesus. It should be carefully noted that the above proclamation of Saint Paul's asserted that those who were "being saved" were the ones who heard and accepted the doctrine; that they must always "stand firm" or "hold fast" to the teaching being delivered; that Saint Paul handed on only what he himself had "received"; that it was all "in accordance with the Scriptures", and was also the substance of what the apostles "preached": they preached a saving faith in the Lordship or Messiahship of Christ and in the efficacy of his sacrifice on the cross for sin and of his resurrection from the dead.

It is always important to remember that this doctrine, or content, of the Catholic faith, to which believers of all generations have been required to give a personal assent of faith or belief, is in no way something hypothetical or theoretical or, most of all, optional. Moreover this doctrine, or content, goes all the way back to the beginning; Christianity is inconceivable without it. Moreover, at the same time as the *kerygma,* or message, was being proclaimed, it was accompanied by a teaching program explaining and amplifying the basic message; this also was true from the earliest times. This teaching was catechesis properly so called; it consisted of explanations and amplifications of the core message, and it was conveyed by the natural and normal methods of human teaching and learning, including the transmission of cognitive content in formal propositions addressed to the mind—although the results or fruits of the whole process were not dependent solely upon this natural and human pedagogy but were also subject to what Saint Paul called "the convincing power of the Spirit" (1 Cor 2:4).

Catechesis—the explanation and amplification of the *kerygma*—amounted to nothing else but the instilling of what came to be called the Creed. The earliest Creeds consisted of a profession of faith, often in question-and-answer form, which the person accepting the faith and being baptized was required to assent to: "I believe . . . " in the content delivered in catechesis. It is absolutely necessary to stress this point here in view of the fact that religious education in the postconciliar years came to be characterized by a kind of "creedless catechesis" that would seem to be a wholly untenable oxymoron, since the Creed is, and always has been, simply essential to any catechesis deserving of the name.

In order to accept the fundamental truth and importance of this fact though, it is not necessary, for example, to imagine that the exact wording of the Apostles' Creed as professed today was always in force and was necessarily used as, according to pious legend, having been composed by the apostles, each of them accounting for one of the twelve articles that make up the Apostles' Creed. As Professor J. N. D. Kelly, again, has noted:

> The conclusion is inescapable that, however anachronistic it may be to postulate fixed credal forms for the apostolic age, the documents themselves testify to the existence of a corpus of distinctively Christian teaching. In this sense at any rate it is legitimate to speak of the Creed of the primitive Church. Nor

was it something vague and nebulous: its main features were clearly enough defined. The Epistles and Gospels are, of course, rarely if ever concerned to set out the faith in its fullness: they rather presuppose and hint at it. Even so, it is possible to reconstruct, with a fair degree of confidence, what must have been its chief constituents.[23]

From all these indications, it is easy to see how pertinent is the use of the Apostles' Creed as one of the principal bases of the Catechism for the Universal Church; it is a usage that literally goes back to the beginnings of the Church, and is perhaps the most common basis for the catechisms produced by the Church in the course of her history. Monsignor Eugene Kevane has summed up the pertinence of this use of the Creed in catechesis as follows:

> The original "Apostles' Creed" is simply the profession of the apostolic faith made by the living apostles in their *kerygma,* and continued by their living successors, in a living magisterium sustained by an action of Almighty God in the Church of His Incarnate Son across the centuries between His coming in humility and His second coming in glory. This profession of the apostolic faith always has had one and the same doctrinal substance, the confession of Jesus as the Lord, set in a characteristic Trinitarian form because the one who is our Lord is the eternal Son of God. This apostolic profession of faith is a *typon didaches,* a pattern of doctrine, a content and norm for catechetical teaching . . . it is simply today what we call the Creed.[24]

The Creed, then, traditionally contained and embodied the doctrine, or content, of Christian catechesis. It was first transmitted orally by preaching and teaching down through the centuries and on through the medieval period. Written catechisms, and the study or memorization of them, only came in with the invention

[23] Ibid., pp. 10–11.

[24] Monsignor Eugene Kevane, *Creed and Catechetics: A Catechetical Commentary on the Creed of the People of God* (Westminster, Md.: Christian Classics, 1975), p. 39. Monsignor Kevane points out in a note that the Greek *typon didaches* (Rom 6:17) is the *formam doctrinae* of the Vulgate, the "rule of teaching" of the New American Bible, and simply "the Creed" of the Jerusalem Bible.

of the printing press in the fifteenth century; before that time it was not economically possible to produce books for mass consumption or study. Thus, the advent of catechisms roughly coincided with the Protestant Reformation, and in fact, it was none other than Martin Luther himself who inaugurated the era of the written catechism; this came with the issuance of his Large Catechism, for the use of pastors and teachers, and his Small Catechism, for the common people and for children. Interestingly enough, the catechetical format utilized by Luther included the Creed, the Lord's Prayer, the Commandments, and the Sacraments (although, needless to say, not the *seven* sacraments). Luther's Small Catechism, which came out in 1529, was in the now-familiar (and lately much-maligned) form of short questions and answers adaptable for rote memorization.[25]

In response to Luther's Large and Small Catechisms, and also to those issued by other Protestant confessions such as John Calvin's Geneva Catechism, Saint Peter Canisius, Jesuit and Doctor of the Church, responded from the Catholic side with his own vastly successful Large and Small Catechisms; these Catholic catechisms were not openly polemical documents but they did seek to refute Protestant errors in the way the questions in them were framed and answered. Saint Peter Canisius was followed by another Jesuit saint and Doctor of the Church, who produced his own Large and Small Catechisms at the very end of the sixteenth century—catechisms that long remained in use, especially in Mediterranean countries. This was Saint Robert Bellarmine.

Meanwhile the Council of Trent, which sat in three sessions between 1545 and 1563, in one of its very first conciliar actions, mandated the preparation of an official Catholic Catechism to be "drawn from Scripture and the Orthodox fathers and containing only matters of faith". This mandate resulted in the famous *Catechismus Romanus,* or, as it is more often called in English, the

[25] See Berard L. Marthaler, OFM Conv., "Catechetical Directory or Catechism: *Une Question Mal Posée*", in Dermot A. Lane, ed., *Religious Education and the Future: Essays in Honor of Patrick Wallace* (Dublin, Ireland: Columba Press, 1986), p. 57.

Catechism of the Council of Trent. It came out in 1566, twenty years after the conciliar decision. Addressed to pastors and teachers, this Catechism was cast in the by then traditional form covering the Creed, the Sacraments, the Decalogue, and the Lord's Prayer. Thus, once again, the plan for the Catechism for the Universal Church takes its place in an honorable line. The Catechism of the Council of Trent served as the foundational Catholic catechism for four hundred years, up to the time of Vatican Council II.[26]

The famous Baltimore Catechism, so long familiar to Americans, was one of many national catechisms produced in various parts of the Church. It came about as a result of the authorization of the American bishops at the Third Plenary Council of Baltimore in 1884. Published in the following year, the Baltimore Catechism, in both its structure and content, drew heavily upon a 1777 Irish Catechism issued by the archbishop of Cashel, which itself went back to the models of Canisius, Bellarmine, and the Catechism of the Council of Trent.[27] According to some accounts, the Baltimore Catechism was never either as popular or as universal as the later mythology about it contended. Apparently it was subject to criticisms in various American dioceses virtually from the time of its first appearance, and some bishops even issued their own catechisms in preference to it.[28] Also, in the American environment, its basic text quickly became transformed in some of the graded religion books, illustrated workbooks, and the like, for which Americans have such a penchant.

Nevertheless, the basic Baltimore Catechism helped form several generations of Catholics in this country during a period when the Catholic faith was most vital and vibrant in the lives of those who professed and tried to live it. Moreover, many of those who were brought up on the Baltimore Catechism will remember that, although there was indeed memorization and plenty of it, memorization was not all that there was. The Baltimore Catechism was

[26] Ibid., p. 59.

[27] Ibid., pp. 61–63.

[28] See Mary Charles Bryce, "The Baltimore Catechism—Origin and Reception", in Warren, ed., *Sourcebook,* pp. 140–45.

almost invariably used in conjunction with supplementary Bible stories, lives of the saints, and the like; and, especially in Catholic schools, there was also regular active involvement in the Mass and the sacraments that complemented the lessons from the Baltimore Catechism. The irrational and sometimes almost violent prejudice that emerged against the Baltimore Catechism in the immediate postconciliar years was surely largely undeserved, for this national catechism did its job very well for its time and circumstances. Only a later mythology growing up around it made possible the almost uniformly negative light in which it is viewed today. It seems likely that this prejudice against the Baltimore Catechism reflects prejudice against the typical manifestations of preconciliar Catholic life and practice generally more than it reflects a balanced judgment about a "catechism". The Baltimore Catechism came to be a symbol of everything some people thought was bad in preconciliar Catholicism in America; included in that, apparently, were propositional formulations of the belief of the Church of any description.

The fact remains, though, that both in form and in content, the "catechism" embodied the Church's typical systematic presentation of her faith to be transmitted. Such things as the question-and-answer format and memorization were part of the Catholic way of life; for four centuries after the Council of Trent they constituted the Church's favored method for handing on her faith. It is not that no efforts were ever made to modify or update the 1566 Catechism of the Council of Trent or the many national, local, or particular catechisms that had stemmed from it; it was just that no alternative to a catechism was ever seriously considered—until the time of the Second Vatican Council.

In 1870 the First Vatican Council debated a *schema* titled "the Compilation and Adoption of a Single Short Catechism for the Universal Church". The debate on this *schema* was quite sharp and constituted something of an object lesson for those who think that there was never any "free speech" in the Church or real, live debate until Vatican II. For many Vatican I bishops opposed this earlier version of a proposed Catechism for the Universal Church;

these bishops believed it was impossible to produce one single religion text for a worldwide, multicultural society; the same argument is still being heard today, of course. Interestingly enough though, these same Vatican I bishops opposed the idea because a single uniform catechism, they thought, would impinge upon the then fairly well established rights of individual bishops to issue their own catechisms if they saw fit—another thought to be pondered by those who think that Catholic bishops were totally subservient to Rome up until Vatican II. "To catechize the people is one of the great duties of a bishop", one Hungarian archbishop declared. "If a catechism is dictated to us, our sermons will be dictated next."

Nevertheless, the *schema* for a Churchwide catechism was actually approved by a majority of the fathers of the First Vatican Council, indeed a majority of four-fifths of the fathers present and voting. However, along with some of Vatican I's other actions, the *schema* was never promulgated, owing to the outbreak of the Franco-Prussian War and the subsequent march on Rome of the Italian national army, which meant that Vatican Council I was unceremoniously interrupted by this military action, never to be resumed.[29]

With the commencement of Vatican II in 1962, there were a number of renewed suggestions that the Vatican I catechism project be revived. Twenty-two requests for a single catechism for the entire Church came in during the preparatory phase of the Council. The Roman Curia actually recommended a kind of master text setting forth all Catholic doctrine, a kind of codification of basic

[29] See Michael Donnellan, "Bishops and Uniformity in Religious Education: Vatican I to Vatican II", in Warren, ed., *Source book,* pp. 238–39. Those today who think that the Catechism will be an imposition on bishops or bishops' conferences wishing to issue their own catechisms must face the fact that the popes—and, for instance, Cardinal Ratzinger—have for years been pleading with the bishops to proclaim the honest doctrine of the Church and to curb dissent. One of the reasons the Catechism for the Universal Church is finally coming into being is because bishops around the world do not have a uniformly good record in this regard, and Rome therefore considers it a duty to move into the vacuum in order to preserve the integrity of Catholic teaching.

teachings (something the American bishops were going to find necessary in 1973, as will be seen). As virtually every history of Vatican II has hastened to record, however, the recommendations of the Roman Curia did not generally fare very well in the course of this twenty-first general council of the Catholic Church.

What finally did come about at Vatican II was the adoption of a recommendation originally made by Bishop Pierre-Marie Lacointe of Beauvais in France. Bishop Lacointe believed that what he called a *"directorium"*, or "directory", setting forth principles and guidelines for the teaching of the faith, was what needed to be prepared; such a directory, he thought, would be preferable to a general, Churchwide catechism.[30]

In any event, this is the course of action the Council followed in the matter. The Vatican II Decree on the Pastoral Office of Bishops in the Church (no. 44) specified that "a directory for the catechetical instruction of the Christian people" be drawn up, "in which the fundamental principles of this instruction and its organization be dealt with". In the preparation of this directory, "due consideration should be given", the Decree specified, "to the views expressed both by the commissions and by the conciliar fathers".[31]

It was as a result of this conciliar decree, then, that the foundational *General Catechetical Directory* (GCD) came to be issued in 1971 by the Congregation for the Clergy in Rome,[32] inaugurating a new era during which for the first time in many centuries there was no model or prototype Churchwide catechism issued by the Holy See on which other catechisms in use could be based, or to which, at any rate, they had to conform; there was no longer any "point of reference" in catechesis, to use the phrase that emerged later. The Council of Trent was finally over in reality. Henceforth there was to be in place something called a "catechetical

[30] Ibid., pp. 238–39.

[31] Vatican Council II, *Christus Dominus,* no. 44.

[32] Sacred Congregation for the Clergy, *General Catechetical Directory* (Washington, D.C.: United States Catholic Conference Publications Office, 1971).

directory" to provide Roman guidance on the subject of catechesis. This was a new kind of document, though, with which traditionally the Church had had little experience. Nobody quite knew for sure what the new GCD was supposed to do or how it was supposed to work in guiding the catechetical enterprise of the Catholic Church.

Further attention must be given to the *General Catechetical Directory* in a subsequent chapter; the GCD has been of central importance to the teaching of the faith in the postconciliar era. However, the era of this single directory governing the catechetical enterprise was destined to be a relatively brief one in the history of the Church—only a mere twenty years elapsed between the time in 1965 when Vatican II established that a directory and not a catechism would be the foundational document for catechesis in the Church and the time in 1985 when the Synod of Bishops mandated another Catechism for the Universal Church after all. It is almost a foregone conclusion that the issuance of this new Churchwide Catechism will at least in some respects restore the situation that existed in the Church for four hundred years after the Council of Trent, for there will again be a model Catechism issued out of Rome.

Why did the unique reign of the GCD in catechesis in the Church turn out to be such a brief one? There is a short answer to this question: *because it continued to be perceived after Vatican II that the faith was not being properly taught.* This statement can only be asserted at this point. Proofs, demonstrations, and illustrations of its truth, in more than one country and at many levels of instruction, will have to be offered in the course of the remainder of this study, and they will be offered. In one sense the catechetical deficiencies of the postconciliar era are the basic theme of the present study. For the years under consideration here saw the emergence of a strange creedless, contentless, noncognitive kind of so-called catechesis; it emerged and persisted in spite of a marked unpopularity among Catholic parents almost from the moment it was first encountered—and also in spite of regular and repeated efforts both by Rome and by the bishops to provide remedies for the very quickly perceived deficiencies of this new catechesis. The considerable and repeated efforts of the hierarchy to correct this faulty kind of religion teaching will be chronicled in Chapter 3. Suffice it to mention here that many of the same deficiencies persist still, in spite of all the efforts made to correct them, obstinately defended by religious education professionals determined that this strange new kind of catechesis must be considered "the state of the art" in the teaching of religion, regardless of what the Church may decree or decide.

It was because basic deficiencies in the teaching of religion continued to be perceived and verified in the postconciliar era, in spite of opposition to them and in spite of official efforts to correct them, that those in authority in the Church finally came to realize that Vatican II's decision to rely on the *General Catechetical Directory* had been insufficient. This decision had not necessarily been wrong in itself; but it put the Church into a situation of being unable to cope adequately with the situation in catechesis that came to exist. Already at the first Synod of Bishops in 1967, even before the GCD had been completed and issued, the question of whether the Church did not need a foundational catechism was raised by a number of bishops who wanted a definite "rule of faith"; however, no action was taken by the Synod at that time.[33]

By 1983, however, after more than a decade of experience with the GCD—coinciding with the deterioration of catechesis during the same period—Cardinal Joseph Ratzinger felt obliged to state at a public conference in France that "it was an initial and grave error to suppress the catechism and to declare obsolete the whole idea of catechisms".[34] It was fitting that it was the prefect of the Congregation for the Doctrine of the Faith who rendered this judgment, for it was "the doctrine of the faith" that was not being transmitted in too much of what passed for the Church's official catechesis. Neither Vatican II nor the GCD itself "suppressed"

[33] Archbishop William Levada, "Catechism for the Universal Church: An Overview", in *Origins,* CNS Documentary Service, March 8, 1990.

[34] Cardinal Joseph Ratzinger, "Sources and Transmission of the Faith", *Communio* 10 (1983): 18, quoted by Marthaler, "Catechetical Directory", p. 65.

catechisms, by the way; on the contrary, the GCD said that the greatest importance must be attached to catechisms issued by the Church (no. 119). Rather, it was the example of Vatican II in not specifically mandating a catechism to replace the *Catechismus Romanus* that was seized upon by the new religious education professionals as being equivalent to "suppressing" catechisms; as in so many other areas, Vatican II was interpreted as having wanted what the new religious education establishment wanted.

From the realization that a new foundational Catechism was going to be necessary after all to the concrete proposal of Cardinal Law at the 1985 Synod was a very short step. By this time the whole idea had become one of those ideas whose time had come—in the minds of those who cared about the integrity of the faith of the Church at least. The new draft Catechism for the Universal Church sent out to all the bishops in November 1989 was the first tangible result of this whole new midcourse change of direction. The principal remaining question for this chapter of the present study is: Why did a group of Catholic scholars assembled by the Woodstock Theological Center on the campus of Georgetown University feel so intensely obliged to mount their symposium and subsequent publications and publicity in an attempt to bring the whole Catechism project into disrepute? What prompted these Catholic scholars to be so critical—intolerant even—of a perfectly legitimate enterprise decided upon by the duly constituted leadership of their own Church after much sober, serious, and responsible reflection on it? What is suddenly so intolerable about the Catholic Church having a Churchwide foundational Catechism as she has had for centuries?

4.

The aims of the present study are in no wise polemical, and hence it is not one of its aims to provide a comprehensive or definitive response to or refutation of the many critical arguments lodged against the Catechism for the Universal Church by the Woodstock group of Catholic scholars. Beyond taking note of the fact that it is scarcely a "scholarly" undertaking to be resorting to press conferences and public contestations in order to make one's points, it is nevertheless worth going on to try to understand the grounds for this opposition to the Catechism. Why should "scholars", in particular, object so strongly to the Church having a basic statement of what she believes? Since these scholars apparently wish to remain "Catholic" scholars—for so they identify themselves—one would have expected more sympathy for and identification with the Church and her current needs.

It is important to mention and comment on at least a few of the objections of these scholars in order to ascertain where they are coming from; and also in order to be able to judge, at least in a broad general sense, how serious or valid their critique of the Catechism really is. Needless to say, the treatment of some of their positions essayed here lays no claim to be either comprehensive or exhaustive; it only aims to be indicative. Those topics to be covered by looking briefly at some of the positions adopted by some of these scholars will include: the Catechism's alleged misuse of Scripture and its supposed failure to take modern scriptural scholarship into account, its asserted failure to distinguish between matters of faith and theological opinion, its supposed failure to take into account recent developments in Catholic moral theology, and its alleged lack of distinctions concerning levels of doctrine or "the hierarchy of truths", as it is called. These points may be considered in order.

Misuse of Scripture.

With regard to the charge that the new draft Catechism for the Universal Church misuses Scripture and fails to take modern scriptural scholarship into account, the following paragraph from one of the contributions to the Woodstock symposium may perhaps be taken as illustrative of the kinds of objections raised against the Catechism under this heading:

> ...despite what Paul or Mark might have actually thought about Jesus, they are quoted as if they had a full-blown

> Nicene Christology. Despite the late and highly developed character of John's Christology, the "I am" statements in this Gospel are taken as verbatim words of Jesus and used to prove his divinity. Scripture texts are strung together in an indiscriminate manner with too little regard for their integrity. Thus, Jesus as the Son of God in a divine transcendent sense is demonstrated by a literal reading of Peter's confession in Mt 16:17, Paul's conversion experience in Gal 1:15–16, Luke's rendition of Paul's preaching in Acts 9:20, as well as Jn 20:31 and I Thes 1:10. On balance, what is going on here is a sophisticated form of proof-texting, familiar from the manual style of theology. Scripture is pressed onto a procrustean bed. It is as though the biblical renewal had never happened.[35]

What can be said about a paragraph such as this? That "what Paul or Mark might actually have thought about Jesus" could possibly *affect* what the Church, with the assistance of the Holy Spirit, has definitively and infallibly *defined* in the way of a "Nicene Christology"? Supposing one really could ascertain what Paul or Mark "actually thought" about Jesus beyond what they said in plain words in their writings in the New Testament—and it is surely impossible in the nature of the case that this could ever be ascertained by the use of the historico-critical or any other exegetical method—could what they "actually thought" affect what the Church has defined, that is, if the Catholic faith is true at all? This is not to assert that nothing could ever be added to the Church's "Nicene Christology"; it is only to assert that the formulation of the Creed as fashioned at Nicaea and at subsequent councils was "from the beginning suitable for communicating [the] revealed truth" of the matter; and remains "forever suitable for communicating this truth to those who interpret [it] correctly", as the Congregation for the Doctrine of the Faith's 1973 Declaration *Mysterium Ecclesiae,* addressing precisely the issue raised by this

[35] Elizabeth A. Johnson, C.S.J., "Jesus Christ in the Catechism", in Reese, ed., *Universal Catechism Reader,* p. 75. Originally published in *America,* March 13, 1990.

Woodstock scholar, expresses it.[36] If the Church's historic formulation of her Nicene Christology was, therefore—at every stage of the development and formulation of this doctrine—"from the beginning" and "forever suitable" to express the truth of the matter, then it remains especially suitable for use in a Catechism, which is by definition a statement of the Church's faith, not of theological or other kinds of opinions about it.

The position of the author quoted here appears to be that discoveries by biblical scholars might possibly alter articles of faith already defined by the Church. The truth of the matter, though, is that while new knowledge about matters pertaining to the faith may be discovered or acquired, this new knowledge cannot alter or abolish articles of faith already established in the Church and handed down.

It should be emphasized that credal (e.g., Nicea) statements are an interpretation of Scripture, in fact the only authorized one. Thus, the Bible can be shown to have a more precise dogmatic meaning than even its authors may have had.

Historically speaking, the Holy Spirit inspired these authors as the principal author and therefore obviously left potentialities which the human authors may not have had consciously in mind when they wrote but which could be drawn out in more explicit formulations by the magisterium of the Church, which is also guided by the Holy Spirit.

Furthermore, the Woodstock writer, following well known conclusions of form-criticism, presupposes that Christology develops in a direction away from the historical facts. But true Christology adheres to the historical facts in the same way as true Christian faith is a knowledge and awareness of certain historical facts.

Rudolph Bultmann claimed to have shown that the "I am" statements of Jesus in the Gospel according to St. John are not

[36] Congregation for the Doctrine of the Faith, Declaration in Defense of the Catholic Doctrine on the Church against Some Present-Day Errors, *Mysterium Ecclesiae,* June 24, 1973.

historical, but Bultmann argued not only from a mistaken notion of faith but also from a mistaken historical methodology and thus he failed to prove this claim. Our Woodstock author is following the same path as Bultmann regarding the "I am" statements of Jesus in John's Gospel and therefore she cannot expect readers to accept without proof either that St. John's Gospel presents "late Christology" or that the "I am" statements of Jesus in this Gospel are not the exact words of Jesus.

Similarly, the reproach against the Catechism's use of the "I am" statements in Saint John's Gospel to "prove" Christ's divinity "despite the late and highly developed character of John's Christology" simply assumes the truth of the scholarship that has supposedly established that Saint John's Christology *is* "late and highly developed". This scholarship is now apparently supposed to constitute some new norm or standard for judging the faith of the Church. What is really pertinent to faith here, though, is the fact that the Church professes, and has always professed, the divinity of Christ; and hence there is nothing at all illegitimate about making use, among other sources, of the "I am" statements in John to illustrate this established divine truth. John's Gospel, after all, is a very important source for the Church's faith, whenever it was written; and, in any case, the "late" character of this Gospel, *pace* the majority opinion of contemporary biblical scholars, cannot simply be assumed. What, for example, if the late Anglican bishop J. A. T. Robinson's now-celebrated book *Redating the New Testament* is to be credited in this manner?[37] Robinson too was a competent biblical scholar, a member of the club, and he came to disagree with the hypothesis that John's is a very late Gospel. Other scholars have similarly questioned the late character of John's Gospel.[38]

Whether the Gospel according to John was written early or late is something scholars may legitimately debate. But it is most

[37] John A. T. Robinson, *Redating the New Testament* (Philadelphia: Westminster Press, 1976).

[38] Claude Tresmontant, *The Hebrew Christ* (Chicago: Franciscan Herald Press, 1989).

emphatically not the case that the scholarly views of one or another school of thought on this and other issues should ever be enshrined in a catechism. This is to misunderstand what a catechism is and should be. Catechisms expound the faith of the Church not the views of any school of thought, no matter how large the majority of scholars behind it. One obvious difficulty of trying to embody the results of the latest scholarship in a catechism is that these results may not be true. For example, the same author being quoted here also reproaches the Catechism for the Universal Church, in another passage, for not presenting the various "Christologies" that modern scholars believe they have discovered in the various Gospels: "Mark's Christology of the misunderstood, suffering Messiah is different from John's Christology of the Word made flesh who calls his disciples", she declares, and further asserts that these Christologies "cannot be harmonized".[39] The short answer to this is that the Church has always been aware of the differing (but *not* incompatible) views of Christ offered by the four Gospels; but this does not affect the Church's duty and responsibility to transmit in a catechism the truth that is Christ—both Word and Messiah. The draft Catechism for the Universal Church does precisely this.

Moreover, to return to the original paragraph quoted above, modern biblical scholarship has discovered nothing that forbids the use of such events as Peter's confession, Paul's conversion experience, Luke's rendition of Paul's preaching in Acts, and so on, to "demonstrate" that Jesus was the Son of God in a "divine transcendent sense". In point of fact, all of these and many other scriptural passages do provide converging and confirmatory evidence, useful and edifying and legitimate as far as they go, for the Church's faith that Jesus *was* the Son of God in a divine transcendent sense. But the Church's actual faith does not depend ultimately upon any one or all of these passages taken together. "The Church does not draw her certainty about all revealed truth from the holy Scriptures alone", according to Vatican II (*Dei*

[39] Johnson, "Christ in the Catechism", p. 74.

Verbum, no. 9). Nevertheless it is quite legitimate for the Catechism to use these scriptural passages as it has used them, just as it is also legitimate for the Church to present these same scriptural passages to the faithful as part of the liturgy of the Word (itself a part of the Church's on-going "catechesis"). Neither this nor any other Church catechism is limited in its presentation of Scripture to what biblical scholarship may believe it has discovered about Scripture, however interesting the conclusions of this scholarship may otherwise be.

For the truth is that the modern "biblical renewal", as important as it is, need *not* have happened as far as the sanctification and salvation of present-day Christians is concerned. The faithful were being sanctified and saved by the Church's faith and sacraments for many, many centuries before the Bible ever came to be studied scientifically. No doubt the Church would be much the poorer today if this biblical renewal had never happened; it has contributed greatly to the modern understanding of the sources of the faith. But scholarship is no substitute for these sources of the faith. God did not leave the salvation of his people to the vagaries of the scholarship of any era, however valuable the modern contribution to the understanding of the Bible may be considered to be. To alter the famous dictum of Saint Ambrose only slightly: *Non in "scientia" complacuit Deo facere salvum populum suum.*

In her use of Scripture the Church is always going to look to her own faith ahead of any scholarship whatsoever; and her own faith affirms her firm belief that the Gospels as they have been handed down tell "the honest truth about Jesus"; or, again: "Holy Mother Church has firmly and with absolute constancy maintained and continues to maintain that the four Gospels . . . whose historicity she unhesitatingly affirms, faithfully hand on what Jesus, the Son of God, while he lived among men, really did and taught for their eternal salvation. . . ."[40] This is what Vatican II teaches on the subject. Scholars claiming to be Catholic, especially since they are generally so prone to invoke the name of Vatican II against

[40] Vatican Council II, *Dei Verbum,* no. 19.

anything perceived as preconciliar or reactionary, ought especially to be paying close attention to what Vatican II says.

As for the accusation of "proof-texting" leveled against the Catechism, Cardinal Ratzinger himself has recognized that "criteria for the use of Scripture in the definitive text" do need to be included in the final version; at the same time, the Cardinal reported to the 1990 Synod that the Catechism does not aim "to be a scientific study of exegesis".[41] This is correct; that is not what a catechism should be. It seems pretty clear, therefore, that the criticisms of the author quoted here on the Catechism's alleged misuse of Scripture are mostly beside the point.

Faith and Theological Opinion.

Another one of the Woodstock Catholic scholars faults the Catechism because, in treating the question of the angels, it treats "their existence [as] a matter of faith". "Biblical scholars", this author, a professor of theology, explains, "are trying to discover to what extent speaking of these created spirits is a culturally conditioned way of describing both God's activity and evil forces outside individual persons, rather than divinely inspired affirmations."[42] What this sentence seems to mean is that some modern scholars apparently doubt that the Bible's references to "created spirits" really serve to establish that these created spirits actually exist; presumably the sacred writers of the Bible only referred to angels because, in their culture, it was still possible to believe in angels, whereas today, the implication seems to be that it is no longer possible to believe in angels.

Also, presumably, once today's scholars finally "discover" the real truth about the existence of the angels, the faith of the Church will no doubt then have to be guided by this new

[41] Cardinal Joseph Ratzinger, "Report to the Synod on the Proposed Catechism for the Universal Church", in *Origins,* CNS Documentary Service, November 8, 1990.

[42] John H. Wright, S.J., "God in the Catechism", in Reese, ed., *Universal Catechism Reader,* p. 63.

discovery. Who knows? Perhaps this author really wants to save the Church from the embarrassment of continuing to believe that angels exist against the whole spirit of the modern world! However, it is not clear what possible "proof" of the actual existence or nonexistence of angels could possibly emerge from scriptural exegesis alone. Moreover, the Church has in fact affirmed the existence of angels for centuries, so it is probably too late to save her from embarrassment.

Surprisingly, in taking his position that angels may not in fact exist, this author is well aware of the fact that the Fourth General Council of the Lateran, in 1215, decided for the Church as follows regarding the existence of created beings: God, Lateran IV declared,

> by his almighty power from the beginning of time made at once (*simul*) out of nothing both orders of creatures, the spiritual and the corporal, that is, the angelic and the earthly, and then (*deinde*) the human creature, who as it were shares in both orders being composed of spirit and body. For the devil and the other demons were indeed created by God naturally good, but they became evil by their own doing. As for man, he sinned at the suggestion of the devil.[43]

The unbiased reader, faced with this particular passage, would probably not find it hard to conclude from it that the Catholic Church believes it to be true that God created spiritual beings (both angels and devils), subhuman corporal beings, and human beings, a unique combination of the two other kinds of beings. Not this Woodstock author, though, who claims instead that "the council was not intending to teach the existence of angels and devils, since at that time no one questioned their existence. The only question was whether evil spirits were creatures of God or independent beings."[44] In other words, according to this profes-

[43] Symbol of the Fourth General Council of the Lateran (1215), in J. Neuner, S.J., and J. Dupuis, S.J., eds., *The Christian Faith in the Doctrinal Documents of the Catholic Church,* rev. ed. (Westminster, Md.: Christian Classics, 1975), p. 16.

[44] Wright, "God in Catechism".

sor of theology, a general council of the Church need not be followed in its teaching about angels and devils because all the while these creatures were possibly only hypothetical beings, or, at any rate, were beings whose existence is questioned today, even if not at the time the council rendered its decision. Apparently the Holy Spirit allows councils, in their solemn decisions, to be deluded by fantasies, especially since nothing "central" to the faith is involved here.

This is no doubt a theological opinion; it may well seem to be a very plausible one to some in the present cultural climate. For the Catholic obliged to bow before "the sacred and certain teaching of the church", however, this theological opinion has been placed out of bounds by another decision of the Church's magisterium rendered subsequent to the action of the Fourth Lateran Council in 1215; this subsequent magisterial decision is a very recent one, as a matter of fact. In 1968, Pope Paul VI, in the very first article of his Credo of the People of God, quite explicitly took up once again the question of the existence of angels and affirmed on behalf of the Church as follows:

> We believe in one God, the Father, the Son, and the Holy Spirit, Creator of what is visible—such as the world where we live out our lives—and of the invisible—such as the pure spirits which are also called angels—and Creator in each man of his spiritual and immortal soul.[45]

God, then, is the "Creator of . . . pure spirits . . . called angels", according to the supreme magisterium of the Church, speaking in the second half of the present century. Now the reproach leveled at the Catechism under the heading currently under consideration is that the document fails to distinguish between matters of faith and theological opinion. Specifically in this instance, it treats the existence of angels as a matter of faith. But it appears that the existence of angels *is* a matter of faith—unless Pope Paul VI's

[45] Pope Paul VI, Credo of the People of God, Profession of Faith Proclaimed by the Holy Father at the Closing of the Year of Faith, Vatican Polyglot Press, June 30, 1968.

Credo of the People of God is not an authentic expression of the Church's magisterium. In a subsequent chapter it will be verified that the existence of angels was one of the things that a special commission of cardinals insisted had to be included in the famous "Dutch Catechism"; the modern magisterium has insisted on continuing to affirm the existence of angels as part of the Church's faith.

What appears to be the real situation here, then, is that the draft Catechism for the Universal Church has included an accepted doctrine of the faith—the existence of angels—and has thereby excluded a currently fashionable opinion to the effect that it is not necessary to insist upon the existence of angels. The opposite of what the Catechism is being accused of is actually the case here; it is not the Catechism that is having difficulty distinguishing between faith and theological opinion, it is the criticizing scholar.

Is too much being made of this single matter of angels, admittedly not a central affirmation of the Catholic faith? Has this one opinion of a competent and reputable scholar been taken out of its proper context, unfairly? The reply to these questions has to be that it was the Woodstock Catholic scholars themselves who singled out the question at their press conference. The scholar whose presentation has been under consideration here was quoted as saying at that press conference: "I'm not really opposed to angels, but I don't want to make them a matter of faith, and that's what the Catechism does."[46] Any impartial observer, however, can only be quite surprised that a professor of Catholic theology should either be unaware that the supreme pastor of the Church reaffirmed the existence of angels as part of the Church's patrimony of faith as recently as 1968; or should hold that a solemn "Profession of the Faith" issued by a supreme pontiff is somehow not a part of the Church's faith. There does not seem to be any third alternative here, and reflection upon that fact inevitably raises the further question of the competence of such a theologian to be commenting on the Catechism of the Universal Church at all. What about his views generally?

[46] *National Catholic Reporter,* February 9, 1990.

Space permits only one further example under this heading. In the same presentation quoted above the same author declares: "The Catechism says almost nothing about on-going or continuous divine revelation."[47] The trouble, again, with this position is that, in the official teaching of the Church, there is no such thing as "on-going or continuous divine revelation" in the sense in which this author appears to understand it; apparently this author is simply not terribly concerned about the teaching of the Church (which again raises the question of what kind of Catholic theologian he could possibly be). The fact of the matter is that the Catechism said nothing about this for the very good reason that the Church does not recognize its existence. Vatican II, once again, is quite plain about the whole thing: "The Christian economy . . . since it is the new and definite covenant, will never pass away, and no new public revelation is to be expected before the glorious manifestation of our Lord Jesus Christ."[48] Thus according to the Church's teaching, revelation, properly speaking, was a definitive and once-and-for-all affair. So little is this accepted in certain quarters today, however, that so-called "on-going revelation" will have to be dealt with more than once in subsequent chapters. Meanwhile, though, it would appear that it is the professor of theology and not the Catechism out of Rome that is confused about the difference between faith and theological opinion.

Recent Developments in Moral Theology.

The most heated controversies since Vatican II have generally been on the subject of moral issues, on which the Church's firm and unvarying teachings have seemed too inflexible for many in these very permissive times. Thus, it is no surprise that the third part of the new draft Catechism for the Universal Church, concerned with moral teachings and the moral life, is

[47] Wright, "God in Catechism".

[48] Vatican Council II, *Dei Verbum,* no. 4.

the part that has been most severely criticized. As Cardinal Ratzinger himself noted in his progress report on the Catechism to the 1990 Synod:

> This part has been a particular target of criticism, often orchestrated. . . . The press has fully played on it. It was to be expected that the mass media would be particularly interested in the moral part, and, since the revised draft proposes to give the entire Catholic doctrine in this field, it is not surprising that it has aroused the same criticism that moral teachings encounter today.[49]

This observation certainly applies to the treatment of the moral part of the Catechism by the Woodstock group of Catholic scholars. In one of the presentations with the title "The Moral Vision of the Catechism", the following paragraph appears:

> The document makes no reference to the developments that have reshaped Catholic moral thinking. The openness to human experience and the "signs of the times," the admission that the magisterium is not omnicompetent in complex moral questions, the crisis among theologians and the laity following Pope Paul VI's *Humanae Vitae,* the worldwide collapse in the practice of frequent confession, fundamental rethinking on the possibility of mortal sin, the increasing independence of the laity from the hierarchical direction in sexual ethics and married life, the retreat from exceptionless, concrete moral norms, the awareness that all magisterial certitudes are historically conditioned, the admission of error in Church teaching on slavery, religious freedom, women, and so on, and the shift from avoiding sin to taking responsible action to combat oppression and injustice. . . . [50]

This is quite a catalogue. However, as moral theologian Monsignor William Smith of Saint Joseph's Seminary in New York has aptly observed about this same paragraph: "That any of these

[49] Ratzinger, "Report on Proposed Catechism".

[50] William C. Spohn, S.J., "The Moral Vision of the Catechism", in Reese, ed., *Universal Catechism Reader,* pp. 137–38. Originally published in *America,* March 13, 1990.

'developments' or, all of them together, are any part of authentic moral teaching is a very different question. It is simply untrue and unfair to say that the Catechism for the Universal Church has ignored these 'developments'; to some extent it has answered most of them—*in the negative.*"[51]

Since a contrary claim has been thrown out here, namely, that all these items do represent "developments" in Catholic moral thinking, it is both useful and probably necessary to run quickly through this list to determine which, if any, of these items truly do represent authentic developments accepted by the Church and not merely by some moral theologians (or even a majority of them). Each item will be numbered and briefly examined in order.

1. "Openness to human experience and 'the signs of the times'." Whenever the accusation of "proof-texting" is leveled against the Catechism, as it frequently is by the Woodstock group, it is impossible not to think of how these same scholars are so prone to fall back on the phrase "the signs of the times" (Vatican II, *Gaudium et Spes,* no. 4). This, of course, is the favorite proof-text from Vatican II; it is incessantly used to justify all kinds of things that are nowhere to be found in the actual teachings of the Council but are favorite hobbyhorses of those who think they should have been included in the Council documents. Probably the only reason this proof-text is not used even more frequently than it is is that those who most like to invoke the Council are usually content not to attempt to quote any text at all in support of their particular theses but simply to rely on "the spirit of Vatican II" to justify whatever position is being advocated. When a text is actually quoted, though, it is as likely as not to be this one about "the signs of the times". Its only possible rival as a proof-text would probably be the first sentence from *Gaudium et Spes* (no. 1) concerning "the joy and hope, the grief and anguish of the men of our time" that are supposed to be shared by the followers of Christ; but this passage has lately fallen out of favor in some

[51] Monsignor William B. Smith, S.T.D., "Life in Christ—Part III of the Draft Universal Catechism", in *Fellowship of Catholic Scholars Newsletter,* June 1990.

quarters since it speaks of "the men of our time" and does not employ the so-called "inclusive language" demanded by the radical feminists (if they do want to use the phrase, though, these feminists are usually as quick simply to change it on their own as they are to change even Holy Scripture). With regard to "the signs of the times", what is usually and most conveniently forgotten, as it is in the paragraph quoted above, is that Vatican II specified that these signs were to be scrutinized "in the light of the Gospel", remembering that Christians are the "bearers of a message of salvation". In no way was Vatican II supposed to have inaugurated an era of mere "openness to human experience", as the Woodstock author quoted above implies. Rather, Christians were supposed to go out into the world with the message of the real Christ as presented by the magisterium of the Church. Pope John XXIII made this very clear in his famous "Opening Speech to the Council".

2. "The admission that the magisterium is not omnicompetent in complex moral questions." There has been no such admission on the part of the Church; the very use of the word "omnicompetent" here is invidious and erroneous, and hence the question is incorrectly posed in any case. As was earlier quoted in part, Vatican II taught that "in forming their consciences the faithful must pay careful attention to the sacred and certain teaching of the Church. For the Catholic Church is by the will of Christ the teacher of truth. It is her duty to proclaim and teach with authority the truth which is Christ and, at the same time, to declare and confirm by her authority the principles of the moral order which spring from human nature itself."[52] It will be noted that this Vatican II teaching explicitly makes the claim that the Church's magisterium is competent to pass judgment not only on those issues related to the revealed moral law of God, but also on those related to the "natural law". This, of course, has been an enormous bone of contention since *Humanae Vitae;* but the Church has not backed down on her claim; nor could she. This does not represent any claim that she is "omnicompetent" in these matters,

[52] Vatican Council II, *Dignitatis Humanae,* no. 14.

of course, but the Church does hold that she reliably teaches moral truth to which Catholics are obliged to assent and put into practice in their lives.

3. "The crisis among theologians and laity following Pope Paul VI's *Humanae Vitae.*" There is, to be sure, a crisis, but it in no way represents any development in Catholic moral thinking. Rather, it represents an abandonment on the part of many Catholics of a part of that "sacred and certain teaching" that was taught for many centuries and that has many times been reaffirmed by the Church's magisterium since the time of *Humanae Vitae*—for example, by Pope John Paul II in his apostolic exhortation *Familiaris Consortio,* issued a year after the 1980 ordinary session of the Synod of Bishops devoted to the family.[53] That Synod itself, of course, strongly reiterated the same teaching as a collegial action, and the Pope has frequently repeated the same teaching in his weekly audiences, addresses, allocutions, and the like. Whenever the American bishops have touched upon the subject, they too have reaffirmed the teaching. The Church, in short, has not changed her teaching on the controverted subject of birth control, in spite of a contrary belief and practice of some Catholics; it is a magisterial teaching that has not changed, is not going to change, and, indeed, cannot change.

4. "The worldwide collapse in the practice of frequent confession." Here again, the issue is the abandonment of a sacramental practice that continues to be valid in the eyes of the Church, not a development of Catholic moral thinking. In his 1984 apostolic exhortation *Reconciliatio et Paenitentia,* Pope John Paul II issued to his brother bishops and to other pastors of souls what he called an "invitation to make every effort to encourage the faithful to make use of this sacrament. I urge them to use all possible and suitable means to insure that the greatest possible number of our brothers and sisters receive the 'grace that has been given to us' through

[53] Pope John Paul II, Apostolic Exhortation *Familiaris Consortio* on the Role of the Christian Family in the Modern World, November 22, 1981, no. 29.

penance for the reconciliation of every soul and of the whole world with God in Christ". So important does John Paul II consider the practice of confession that in this same apostolic exhortation he declared, speaking of priests, that the whole of a priest's sacerdotal existence

> suffers an inexorable decline if by negligence or for some other reason he fails to receive the Sacrament of Penance at regular intervals and in a spirit of genuine faith and devotion. If a priest were no longer to go to confession or properly confess his sins, his *priestly being* and his *priestly action* would feel its effects very soon, and this would also be noticed by the community of which he was the pastor [emphasis in the original].[54]

Thus, although it may unfortunately be a fact of life in the Church of the present day that there has been a falling off in the regular practice of confession, the Church nevertheless continues to hope and expect that the current situation will be only a temporary one. The Church goes on, and will go on, encouraging recourse to more frequent confession in spite of what the current fashion happens to be.

5. "Fundamental rethinking on the possibility of mortal sin." There certainly has been much "rethinking" on the subject of mortal sin in recent years, but, once again, the Church has not accepted most of this rethinking. In 1975, the Congregation for the Doctrine of the Faith in Rome issued a Declaration on Certain Questions Concerning Sexual Ethics, *Persona Humana,* which devoted considerable space to this very same topic in what was otherwise a relatively short document. *Persona Humana* rejected what it called "the current tendency to minimize, when not denying outright, the reality of grave sin, at least in people's actual lives". The Declaration went on to reject also the so-called "fundamental option" theory, whereby a person only sins mortally (commits a sin that brings about his separation from God) by a fundamental adverse decision against God that totally commits

[54] Pope John Paul II, Apostolic Exhortation *Reconciliatio et Paenitentia* on Reconciliation and Penance, December 2, 1984, no. 31.

the whole person; and then it went on to specify that a person "sins mortally not only when his action comes from direct contempt for love of God and neighbor, but also when he consciously and freely, for whatever reason, chooses something which is seriously disordered".[55] A decade later, in *Reconciliatio et Paenitentia,* Pope John Paul II reaffirmed the same reality of mortal sin in almost the same words; the Holy Father then went on to assert that one's "fundamental orientation can be radically changed by individual acts".[56] So much, then, for the "rethinking" of the "possibility" of the commission of mortal sins as far as the Church is concerned. Mortal sin is real, and nothing contemporary moral theologians have come up with or might come up with can possibly change that reality.

6. "The increasing independence of the laity from hierarchical direction in sexual ethics and married life." To the extent that the Catholic laity have indeed declared their independence from "hierarchical direction" (read: "the law of Christ") in matters of sex and marriage, then to that same extent they have taken to acting upon something resembling Protestant "private judgment" rather than forming their consciences in accordance with the mind of the Church. These laity may think they still continue to profess the Catholic faith; the Church's own teachings on the matter, however, give no support to this new way of looking at magisterial teachings. *Persona Humana,* already quoted above, specifies both that no one can "make value judgments according to his personal whim" and that "the moral goodness of the acts proper to the conjugal life . . . does not depend solely on sincere intentions or on an evaluation of motives". This same Declaration reaffirms the Church's constant teaching that "every genital act must be within the framework of marriage".[57] Thus, a declaration of independence from "the hierarchy" on matters of sex and

[55] Congregation for the Doctrine of the Faith, Declaration on Certain Questions concerning Sexual Ethics, *Persona Humana,* December 29, 1975, no. 10.

[56] John Paul II, *Reconciliatio et Paenitentia,* no. 18.

[57] Congregation for Doctrine of Faith, *Persona Humana,* nos. 3, 5, and 7.

marriage really means a declaration of independence from the Catholic Church and her moral teachings—if it remains true, and it surely does, that to be a Catholic one must accept and try to put into practice what the Church teaches with the help of God's grace. Those Catholics who have come to have a different idea about this are not truly living in accordance with what is required by their profession of faith.

7. "The retreat from exceptionless, concrete moral norms." Once again, *Persona Humana* is the official Church document that teaches that "those . . . people are in error who today assert that one can find neither in human nature nor in the revealed law any absolute and immutable norm to serve for particular actions. . . ."[58] The Church has not retreated from her position upholding the existence of exceptionless, concrete moral norms; nor will she retreat.

8. "The awareness that all magisterial certitudes are historically conditioned." Of course they are historically conditioned in the sense of being products of their own time, reflecting the degree of knowledge and understanding of their own time. This is not, however, to say that they are less than true with regard to the questions they address and answer. Here the statement already quoted from the Holy See's Declaration *Mysterium Ecclesiae* applies, namely, that "magisterial certitudes" of whatever era, provided they are authentic, "remain forever suitable for communicating . . . truth".[59]

9. "The admission of error in Church teaching on slavery." There was not so much "error" in the Church's teaching about slavery as there was a practical failure on the Church's part to apply her teachings on justice to the widespread social evil of slavery, as Vatican II finally did so creditably (*Gaudium et Spes,* no. 29).

10. "The admission of Church error on . . . religious freedom." There has been no admission of error by the Church in the matter

[58] Ibid., no. 4.

[59] Congregation for Doctrine of Faith, *Mysterium Ecclesiae.*

of her teaching on religious liberty for the simple reason that there was no such error. In the Vatican II Declaration on Religious Liberty, *Dignitatis Humanae,* the Church taught that "the human person has a right to religious freedom" in the sense of being free from "coercion" and never "forced to act against his convictions in religious matters in private or in public by any external power"; at the same time, internally, according to the same Council document, "all men are bound to seek the truth, especially in what concerns God and his Church ... [and] these obligations bind man's conscience". The council's teaching, in other words, had to do with "freedom from coercion"; it left "intact the traditional Catholic teaching on the moral duty of individuals towards the true religion and the one Church of Christ".[60]

References to "error" having been corrected by this Vatican II teaching on religious freedom generally have reference to nineteenth-century condemnations by Pius IX and Leo XIII of then current ideas of a kind of "freedom of conscience" that claimed autonomy for the human conscience and held that it was subject to no law outside itself. To understand correctly both what Vatican II affirmed and what the nineteenth-century popes condemned—it was not the same thing—it is necessary to distinguish the various meanings of popular phrases such as "religious freedom" and "freedom of conscience". The necessary distinctions were made clear on the floor at Vatican II. Bishop Emile DeSmedt of Bruges, who introduced the *schema* that became the Declaration on Religious Liberty,[61] aptly quoted Pope Pius XI who had distinguished between "freedom of consciences" (plural)—meaning what Vatican II meant and affirmed, namely, that people had a right to freedom from coercion in religious matters—and "freedom of conscience" (singular), allowing for an absolute independence of the human conscience from any law, human or divine, which Pius XI, echoing his nineteenth-century predecessors, rightly called

[60] Vatican Council II, *Dignitatis Humanae,* nos. 2, 1.

[61] Bishop Emile DeSmedt, "Address Introducing Draft on Religious Liberty", in Floyd Anderson, ed., *Council Daybook: Vatican II* (Sessions 1 and 2) (Washington, D.C.: National Catholic Welfare Conference, 1965), pp. 277–82.

"absurd". This distinction was clearly brought out and explained to the Council fathers by Bishop DeSmedt in one of the Council's major interventions; the fathers could not but have known exactly what they were voting for when they approved Vatican II's Declaration on Religious Liberty, and, in their minds, they certainly did not believe they were correcting any past "error" in Church teaching on religious freedom. In view of the history of this matter, available to everybody, it is not only unscholarly to continue talking about a "change" in Church teaching on religious freedom at Vatican II, it bespeaks either ignorance of the true facts or unwillingness to face them.

11. "The admission of error in Church teaching on . . . women." Once again, the Church has not taught any error on the subject of women and hence has not admitted to any such error. The continuing attacks of the radical feminists and their allies on the Church's "patriarchy" ought to be proof enough that the Church has in no way changed her teaching regarding women and their place in God's plan. It is not even clear, in fact, what this Woodstock author had in mind by including this item in his list of things that have supposedly been reshaping Catholic moral thinking. To judge by what this and some of the other Woodstock authors think about things in general, and the Holy See's recent reaffirmations of many Church teachings in particular, it is not likely that many of these authors would favor the treatment of women to be found, for example, in Pope John Paul II's 1988 apostolic letter *Mulieris Dignitatem* on the dignity and vocation of women. However that may be, this is the latest thing on what the Church truly teaches about women.[62] And it does not contain any error, regardless of what today's radical feminists may think about it.

12. "The shift from avoiding sin to taking responsible action to combat oppression and injustice." At the risk of sounding monotonous, it is once again necessary to point out that there has not been

[62] Pope John Paul II, Apostolic Letter of the Supreme Pontiff on the Dignity and Vocation of Women on the Occasion of the Marian Year, *Mulieris Dignitatem,* August 15, 1988.

any such "shift" in Catholic moral thinking as the one described here. Vatican II, *inter alia,* taught that "man is prone to evil" and that "inducements to sin . . . can only be overcome by unflinching effort under the help of grace".[63] And, in a passage that seems especially pertinent to any "scholarly" claim that the Church's view of sin might somehow have been changed, Pope John Paul II, in *Reconciliatio et Paenitentia,* already quoted above, spoke as follows:

> While every sincere and prudent attempt to clarify the psychological and theological mystery of sin is to be valued, the Church nevertheless has a duty to remind all scholars in this field of the need to be faithful to the word of God that teaches us about sin. She likewise has to remind them of the risk of contributing to a further weakening of the sense of sin in the modern world.[64]

Once again, there has been no "shift" away from sin on the Church's part, and one can only wonder how the Woodstock author under consideration here could have come to believe this and the other assertions he has made regarding supposed new "developments" that have allegedly "reshaped" Catholic moral thinking. The developments cited are not developments and have reshaped nothing Catholic. It seems evident that this author simply inhabits a different universe of moral discourse than the one assumed and expounded in the teaching documents of the Church; once again, therefore, it appears that this writer is incompetent to say what Catholic moral teaching is or otherwise comment upon it; it would seem to follow from this that his comments upon the moral part of the Catechism of the Universal Church are irrelevant.

Distinctions concerning "the Hierarchy of Truths".

In his progress report on the draft Catechism to the 1990 Synod, Cardinal Ratzinger noted that a recurring criticism of the text,

[63] Vatican Council II, *Gaudium et Spes,* no. 25.

[64] John Paul II, *Reconciliatio et Paenitentia,* no. 17.

which has had a wide echo in the secular press, is that the text does not properly respect "the hierarchy of truths". The Cardinal confessed to a degree of puzzlement about this particular criticism: "It is not always easy to know what everyone means by this formula and even less to find clear guidelines as to the manner of accomplishing it."[65]

The Woodstock group of Catholic scholars similarly made much of this issue. It was one of their prime issues, mentioned in press stories about their symposium.[66] At their press conference, one of their representatives spoke out with respect to this subject: "Everything is presented on the same level of credibility, whether it's a matter of faith or a matter of theological evaluation."[67]

This particular scholar provided a clue to what was really being aimed at, however, when speaking at greater length in his presentation reprinted in the *Universal Catechism Reader* as a practitioner of catechetics looking at the draft Catechism. He wrote:

> The Church sorely needs some way of distinguishing infallible from noninfallible teaching. This is notably absent from the universal Catechism. Failure to make this distinction has been leading to great confusion among catechists and the children they teach. If all teachings bear the same weight, when some are changed—as happened with various reforms after the Second Vatican Council (vernacular language, altar facing the people, no abstinence on Fridays, more frequent annulments)—then all appear arbitrary. The Catechism must make clear what teachings cannot ever be changed because they are matters of Christian faith.[68]

It should be noted that none of the examples offered here by this author are "teachings" at all; all are matters of Church discipline or practice, which most catechists teach as being changeable by Church law in a way that "teachings" are not changeable. How

[65] Ratzinger, "Report on Proposed Catechism".

[66] *Washington Times*, January 29, 1990.

[67] *National Catholic Reporter*, February 9, 1990.

[68] Francis J. Buckley, S.J., "Children and the Catechism", in Reese, ed., *Universal Catechism Reader*, pp. 191–92.

is it that these liturgical and penitential practices, which everybody knows changed after Vatican II, are suddenly brought in by this author to illustrate a supposed lack of distinctions in the Catechism concerning "the hierarchy of truths"? Why does the author use these particular illustrations to try to make the point that the Church (and the Catechism) need to distinguish "infallible" from "noninfallible" teaching? What is this author trying to get at here?

Cardinal Ratzinger's report to the 1990 Synod on the progress of the Catechism project provides a clue to what the real underlying issue may be here. In dealing with the many criticisms about the supposed failure of the Catechism to distinguish among the Church's hierarchy of truths, the Cardinal declared that the completed Catechism would include "references to the levels of authority of documents of the magisterium (avoiding theological notes, but making a distinction in Christian doctrine between *that which is essential and that which is derived*)" (emphasis added).[69]

Thus, there is a hierarchy of truths to be distinguished. Vatican II clearly teaches that "there exists an order or 'hierarchy' of truths since they vary in relation to the foundation of the Christian faith".[70] The rank or position of a given truth within this hierarchy, according to Vatican II, would seem to be based on its *"relation to the foundation"* of the faith as a whole. Similarly, Cardinal Ratzinger distinguished between doctrine "which is *essential* and that which is *derived*". Neither Vatican II nor Cardinal Ratzinger, in other words, made their distinction between doctrine that is essential and doctrine that, supposedly, is *non*essential; that kind of distinction does not figure in their thinking. This is not true, however, of the thinking of the Woodstock author.

This scholar, in complaining about the failure of the Catechism to distinguish properly among the Church's hierarchy of truths, sees the whole issue in very different terms than Vatican II or Cardinal Ratzinger; he is concerned with distinctions between

[69] Ratzinger, "Report on Proposed Catechism".

[70] Vatican Council II, *Unitatis Redintegratio,* no. 11.

teachings that are infallible and those that are noninfallible, and he appears to equate the latter with teachings that may be *changed,* just as liturgical and penitential discipline and the like were changed after Vatican II. He never managed to identify any *teaching* that was changed after Vatican II; nevertheless he managed to identify *change,* and that, for him, was the important thing (and for those who have a new vision of the faith different in a number of really substantial respects from the faith handed down from the apostles). Just as Friday abstinence and the language of the Mass were changed after Vatican II, so, presumably, can "Nicene Christology", say, be changed by the discovery of variant "Christologies" in the four Gospels; or perhaps the Church's millenial belief in angels may be dropped in response to the current *Zeitgeist;* or the affirmation of the existence of exceptionless, concrete moral norms be abandoned in accordance with a new consensus among scholars.

The expectation seems to be, indeed, that anything not infallibly defined by the Church is now up for grabs and can be altered if sufficient reason to do so exists in the minds of modern scholars and experts. This appears to be the viewpoint of all the Woodstock scholars examined here; it also just happens to be the position of the theological dissenters from the encyclical *Humanae Vitae* back in 1968: if a teaching is not infallible, it must be fallible; and if it is fallible, it must be changeable. One of the basic ideas seems to be that the Catholic faith really consists of a body of truths yet to be discovered or, at any rate, to be elucidated authoritatively by means of scholarly and scientific methods applied by—who else? —scholars such as themselves. In truth they do not seem to be able to distinguish what a "teaching" actually is or get the meaning of the word "Catholic" right; nevertheless they are not deterred. The Catholic faith, in their view, is not something revealed once and for all that is also definite and knowable, handed down and authentically interpreted by a living magisterium of pope and bishops, ordained successors of Peter and the other apostles of Jesus, enjoying the special assistance of the Holy Spirit in the exercise of their office. This may well represent the Church's own view of herself (it does), but it is surely not the viewpoint upon which these scholars are basing their criticisms of the draft Catechism for the Universal Church.

Most of these authors may well accept, of course, such broad and traditional beliefs as that the faith of the Church is based upon a revelation of Jesus delivered to his disciples; but on the evidence that has been examined here they also appear to see themselves as both entitled and competent to examine the faith of the Church according to criteria determined by them and according to the canons of their respective scholarly disciplines—even against, if necessary, official interpretations that happen to be provided by the magisterium of the Church. Nor does there appear to be any appeal or recourse from the judgments they render.

These scholars also apparently see themselves as both entitled and competent to decide when the current variant beliefs of some members of the Church—such as, for example, what some Catholics today erroneously believe about the nonexistence of angels or the licitness of contraceptive use—must supersede what the official magisterium continues to hold. No wonder they want distinctions between "core" Catholic beliefs and "less essential" ones! They appear to want to be able to throw out some beliefs entirely! They not only have another agenda, they have another conception of the Catholic faith.

All of this represents a very different conception of "the hierarchy of truths" than the one assumed and described by Vatican II and Cardinal Ratzinger. In no way does the Cardinal appear to see the issue in terms of "more essential" and "less essential" beliefs, but rather in terms of primary and derivative beliefs. The critics and the Cardinal are talking about two different conceptions. No wonder the Cardinal found it "not always easy to know what everyone means by this formula" of the hierarchy of truths. It probably never entered his mind that the basis of some of the criticism of the Catechism for treating everything on the same level was really aimed at preventing the Catechism from presenting as a matter of faith anything that modern scholars have decided should not be a matter of faith but rather should be subject to change or abandonment if these scholars so decree. Acceptance of such a point of view would be tantamount, of course, to recognizing scholars as a new Church magisterium (or co-magisterium); it goes without saying that any Church in which scholars and experts were thus recognized to be the arbiters and doctors of the faith would necessarily be a very different entity from the Catholic Church that has in fact come down from the apostles.

5.

The vision of the Woodstock group of Catholic scholars critical of the new draft Catechism for the Universal Church, as it has emerged from the samples of their thinking scrutinized here, is a very different vision from the one embodied in the Church's magisterial documents with which the views of the Woodstock group have been compared. It goes without saying, therefore, that the Woodstock vision is very different from the one the Church is attempting to embody in the new Catechism, since this document, by definition, is not supposed to contain anything else but the teachings of the Church as they are found in Scripture, Tradition, and the magisterial documents of the Church.

Recognizing these fundamental differences, the question inevitably arises as to what qualifications or suitability these scholars have to be critiquing and passing judgment on a Church Catechism, considering that they do not even recognize what a catechism is supposed to be—a basic statement of the Church's faith as handed down and interpreted by the magisterium—and considering too that they do not appear to accept the Church's own account of her faith as set forth in her various teaching documents. Certainly the question becomes pertinent of just who is really responsible for causing "confusion and division" in the Church—those who are attempting to set forth the Church's faith in response to an official commission, or those who find it imperative to promote another and different version of the faith than the official one, meanwhile arrogating to themselves the right to do this.

The seriousness of what has taken place here—and what is at stake here—is not confined to the scandal of a group of self-appointed scholars publicly attacking a Church process and product; the seriousness of it all is also revealed by the standpoint from which they have chosen to launch their attack: they deny the hierarchy the right in practice to issue any document not reviewable by them. They are thus, in effect, setting themselves up as a kind of substitute or rival hierarchy or magisterium. If the bishops will not listen to them—and ultimately, of course, they will not, especially (but not only) because Rome is always there—then perhaps the faithful among the public at large will listen to them; and, given the state of modern culture, some may just find their novel account of the faith more to their liking than the official one that the bishops received from their predecessors and are obliged to hand on to their successors. Thus it was essential to the whole Woodstock enterprise to "go public"; the Woodstock scholars have no chance of achieving their goal of establishing a new version of the faith in any other way.

What has taken place here is much more serious than the fact that someone has publicly criticized the Church. The Church can take criticism if it is truly just criticism and not an attempt to alter in some crucial respects what she believes and holds. The Church commonly gets plenty of criticism, too! Indeed, once the preparation process for the Catechism was finally brought out into the open from its earlier *sub secreto* status—owing in part to the initiatives taken by the Woodstock group—other critics and scholars entirely loyal to the Church were found to be quite critical of the present draft Catechism in many respects. This was entirely as it should be; it had never been claimed that the draft was perfect; the plan was always to consult the bishops of the world, who, as the Church's official teachers, would respond with the appropriate criticisms and suggestions for improvement.

Once everybody else had gotten into the act, however, even the loyal and pro-magisterium Fellowship of Catholic Scholars (FCS) devoted two complete issues of its quarterly *FCS Newsletter* to the draft Catechism; while much was found to be praised in the document, much was found to be criticized as well.[71] For example, Father Ronald Lawler, O.F.M. Cap., wrote as follows about what he called the Catechism's "flaws in certain specific matters":

> There are, in fact, a surprising number of important flaws in this draft. Often it fails to provide what one most basically expects of a catechism: a clear statement of what the Church teaches, defining clearly what the Church defines clearly, making distinctions that the Church makes in her official documents, presenting precisely the message the Church herself has provided. The authors of a catechism must work with a certain austere self-denial: when there are diverse positions clearly legitimate in the Church, they must not present as Church teaching the views they themselves prefer. And when the Church insistently teaches things that are likely to be assailed the devoted catechist does not for a moment consider stating faith with less force and clarity than the witness of the Church demands. The authors of this draft do not always succeed in this.[72]

So criticism, as such, is not the main issue here. Indeed, the American bishops themselves sent in a report on the Catechism that was quite critical of the draft. When the provisional text of the Catechism arrived, Archbishop Daniel E. Pilarczyk of Cincinnati, the current president of the National Conference of Catholic Bishops (NCCB), appointed an ad hoc review committee of bishops whose initial purpose was to provide some assistance to the individual bishops who would presumably be sending in their contributions. Subsequently, a request was received from the Holy See for a conference response to the draft, which this ad hoc committee was then able to provide.[73]

[71] *Fellowship of Catholic Scholars Newsletter,* June and September 1990.

[72] Father Ronald Lawler, O.F.M. Cap., S.T.D., "Life in Christ—Part III of the Draft Universal Catechism", in ibid., June 1990.

[73] The ad hoc American bishops' committee for the Catechism was composed of Archbishop Oscar J. Lipscomb of Mobile, Alabama, chairman; Archbishop Francis B. Schulte of New Orleans, chairman of the bishops' Committee on Education; Archbishop J. Francis Stafford of Denver, chairman

According to this conference response, the American bishops went on record as saying that "the concept of a Catechism for the Universal Church is necessary and useful for catechesis in the Church"; they added (which was surely not required if they were not really sincere) that "the text is well written and often eloquent", and they also praised "the orientation of the compendium to the Second Vatican Council and the extensive use of the council documents".[74] The bishops went on to point out, however, that the time allotted for consultation was insufficient; this was undoubtedly the case. As was noted earlier though, this was not because of devious Roman maneuvering but because both Pope John Paul II and Cardinal Ratzinger had sincerely wanted and hoped for a finished product by the time of the 1990 Synod, the twenty-fifth anniversary of Vatican II. This proved to be impossible in the end. At the 1990 Synod, therefore, Cardinal Ratzinger indicated that the new target date for the finished Catechism was henceforth to be 1992.[75] Whether this new date will be met remains to be seen as of the time of this writing. (The American bishops, by the way, also wanted the name of the document changed to "A Compendium of Catholic Doctrine for the Preparation of Catechisms", but the Commission for the Catechism did not accept this suggestion.)[76]

In some respects, the U.S. bishops' conference report sent to Rome was as critical of individual features of the Catechism as *The Universal Catechism Reader.* In some cases, the bishops made virtually the same criticisms: the bishops too wanted the Catechism to

---

of the bishops' Committee on Ecumenical and Interreligious Affairs; Archbishop John F. Whealon of Hartford, chairman of the bishops' Committee on Pastoral Research and Practices; Bishop Joseph P. Delany of Fort Worth, chairman of the bishops' Committee on Liturgy; and Bishop John R. Keating of Arlington, Virginia, chairman of the bishops' Canonical Affairs Committee. The full text of the committee's report is to be found in *Origins,* CNS Documentary Service, April 26, 1990.

[74] Ibid.

[75] Ratzinger, "Report on Proposed Catechism".

[76] See note 73 supra.

do greater "justice to the biblical scholarship of the last 50 years" and to "reflect the positive insights of contemporary biblical exegesis"; they too criticized the Catechism's lack of what were called proper distinctions "among the levels of doctrines, or the so-called hierarchy of truths", and they also wanted the text to "show clearly what is essential to the Catholic faith".[77] The bishops seem to have been more than a little influenced by some of the current received ideas of theologians in the United States, some of which, as has been shown above, are not exactly helpful. Yet the spirit in which the criticisms of the bishops were offered—a spirit consciously favorable to the issuance of a Catechism for the Universal Church—meant that the effect of their criticisms was totally different from the effect of the Woodstock assault aimed at undermining the credibility of the whole Catechism enterprise, bringing the document into disrepute before it could even be issued in final form. Nevertheless, given the radical negativism of the Woodstock attack, it does seem somewhat strange that the bishops do not seem to be nervous about the company they find themselves in with respect to some of the criticisms they have offered. How important, really, is even the best and the most sound of biblical exegesis, which in its nature is so often esoteric, to catechesis, the imparting of the simple, basic faith of the Church?

Similarly, the persistence of concern about the theme of the hierarchy of truths no doubt has its importance, but, again, in a catechism? The fact is that past Church catechisms did *not* generally distinguish among the hierarchy of truths. As one study concluded about the authors of earlier catechisms: "The authors of catechisms attempted to draw up as systematic an explanation of Christian belief as possible, which summarized the whole of Catholic teaching. Although the authors were systematic in presentation, *they did not differentiate the hierarchy of truths*" (emphasis added).[78] Why, then, is such a differentiation suddenly required today? Whose agenda is served most by insisting on this point? To the extent that today's

[77] Ibid.

[78] Donnellan, "Bishops and Uniformity", p. 233.

concern about this subject reflects even an unspoken assumption that some beliefs are less important and hence can safely be dissented from, then, this represents a profoundly aberrant understanding of what faith is supposed to be. The faith is proclaimed so that it can be believed; it is the good news! Cutting and trimming to establish what parts of it perhaps do not have to be believed is to undermine the whole enterprise of faith; it is antithetical to the essence of faith: "I assure you that whoever does not accept the reign of God like a little child shall not take part in it" (Mk 10:15).

However, this does not appear to be a really fundamental flaw in the case of the bishops' conference report on the Catechism; for in other parts of their report, the bishops clearly affirm the necessity of believing the whole content of the faith and they even make a rather telling criticism of one element surprisingly absent from the draft Catechism: "The text speaks of giving assent to the extraordinary magisterium", the bishops' conference report notes, "but ignores the ordinary teaching of pope and bishops."[79] Considering that this has been the precise point at issue in the matter of the theological dissent that has raged in the Church since *Humanae Vitae*—whether Catholics may or may not legitimately dissent from authoritative Church teachings that are merely "ordinary"—it is both surprising that the draft Catechism failed to address the issue and praiseworthy that the American bishops did address the issue and provide the correct answer to it in accordance with *Lumen Gentium*, no. 25.

Mere criticism of the Catechism as such, then, is not the problem; it was the duty and responsibility of the bishops to criticize it in the instance just cited. There does remain a problem, though, and it is twofold; it comprises (1) the kind of public criticism of the Catechism that undermines its credibility with the faithful (and also, not incidentally, undermines the authority of the Church in general), and (2) the kind of criticism that arises out of premises and assumptions that deviate from the faith of the Church as set forth in her magisterial documents. Neither

[79] See note 73 supra.

of these kinds of criticism is present in the report prepared by the ad hoc committee on the Catechism, however critical it may be in some respects; both kinds of criticism overwhelmingly characterize the critique offered by the Woodstock group of Catholic scholars in their symposium, press conferences, articles, book, and so on.

At a public meeting of what was called the Woodstock Forum held on November 28, 1990, at Georgetown University—a meeting apparently held to celebrate the publication of the book *The Universal Catechism Reader*—several of the actual Woodstock authors turned out to "entertain" a large and appreciative audience, presumably made up of Catholics (since otherwise why would they come to a "forum" on a subject such as the Catechism?). The verb "entertain" is deliberate, for that was the prevailing atmosphere of the meeting. The Woodstock authors made it clear that they "had not come to praise" the Catechism; overtones of what they then continued to term their own "Shakespearian language", several times repeated like a *Leitmotiv,* caused titters all night long. Actual laughter greeted such ideas as the characterization of "Christ going around being submissive to his Father" or that of "the Christian presenting an unblotted copybook or clean slate at the Last Judgment" (when was the last time any of these people participated in an Easter Vigil with its powerful symbolism of the white garment presented to the baptizands and confirmands?).

The substantive points lodged against the draft Catechism at the Woodstock Forum have been adequately sampled (and answered) earlier. What was most salient about this public meeting itself was the clubby, in-group atmosphere of assumed and shared condescension that prevailed toward the institutional Church and her continuing backwardness when compared to the sophistication that characterized this meeting. The typical questions from the audience at the end indicated the general level of the whole gathering: "How could the pope and the bishops have been so stupid as to try to issue such a Catechism?" One answer: "The exclusion of current theological scholarship is too consistent to be accidental." Another answer: "This Catechism is clearly an instrument of the 'restoration' "!

Other questions from the audience: "How can the thing be headed off?" "Why don't the American bishops revolt?" Answer to the latter question (sadly): "Less than ten per cent of the bishops responding were negative."

Yet another question from the audience: "What is to be done?" Answer (from the same author who scored "zero" above in enumerating the supposed new "developments" in "Catholic moral thinking"): "The Catechism will be accepted in different ways. There will not be an open rejection of it, but if it is not helpful, it will be put on the shelf. Old Church documents never die; they just gather dust. Just as in the case of *Humanae Vitae, a teaching is not taught unless it is received*" (emphasis added).

This last formulation appears to summarize the fundamental position: it is perfectly clear how these people are oriented; the Church has a right to teach only what they are prepared to accept and endorse. This goes considerably farther even than, say, Protestant "private judgment"; these people do not accept *"Scriptura"*, *"sola"* or otherwise, or any other standard beyond their own assertions of how things are henceforth to be.

These citations must suffice in order to give the flavor of this particular public meeting held at Georgetown University and also to indicate the true agenda of the Woodstock group of scholars in case any doubt remains. Father Thomas J. Reese, S.J., moderator of this forum as well as editor of *The Universal Catechism Reader,* in his introductory remarks at the meeting, indicated that the remote origin of the whole Woodstock "pre-emptive strike" against the Catechism for the Universal Church actually went back to the 1985 Synod of Bishops that Father Reese covered as a journalist. Thus it now seems an established fact that the Woodstock group were indeed "laying for" the Catechism all along, from the time it was first mandated by the 1985 Synod as a matter of fact. Father Reese also informed the audience that Pope John Paul II himself had "asked for consultations with bishops and experts", thus strongly implying to this meeting that the Woodstock scholars too had been included in this request for consultations and thus were legitimate participants and were doing nothing improper nor intruding where they did not belong by their multimedia savaging of the Catechism.[80]

If this is true, if the Woodstock scholars were indeed officially asked in some way to participate in the consultations on the Catechism, then this fact was entirely unknown to Father Christoph von Schönborn, O.P., secretary to the official committee of writers of the Catechism. In the spring of 1990, the present writer attended a conference at which Father von Schönborn delivered "A Report on the Universal Catechism". In conversation he expressed himself as being quite disturbed at the anti-Catechism articles that had recently appeared in *America* and *Commonweal* magazines, and he wondered how "the Georgetown Jesuits" could ever have permitted such an anti-Church initiative (Father von Schönborn apparently had no clear idea of the Woodstock Theological Center as an entity separate from Georgetown University). As I reported at the time on Father von Schönborn's reaction:

> . . . he expressed his surprise that sections of the provisional text . . . were quoted in periodical articles. . . . He stated that doing so was explicitly against the *sub secreto* nature of the document as well as a violation of the copyright which belongs solely and exclusively to the Holy See. He characterized such actions as unfair and further observed that the readers of the articles could not verify the criticisms of the various sections since the readers could not have had the embargoed text before them! He indicated that criticism can be helpful but not when it is motivated by a desire to exert pressure on popular opinion against the very idea of a Universal Catechism. These are totally unfair and counterproductive initiatives.[81]

Father von Schönborn was right. The Woodstock attack on the Catechism for the Universal Church was not a legitimate ecclesial

[80] This entire account of the Woodstock Forum of November 28, 1990, is based upon the notes taken down by a knowledgeable observer present at the meeting; these notes are available for scrutiny in the case of a serious inquiry, as is the participant, to discuss what he saw and heard at this public meeting.

[81] Monsignor Michael J. Wrenn, "A Note on the Universal Catechism", in *Fellowship of Catholic Scholars Newsletter,* June 1990.

act but an open anti-ecclesial act. The theologians and scholars who perpetrated it are in open revolt against the Church and what the legitimate authorities of the Church have ordained. If their outlook and approach are allowed to persist—not "prevail", but merely "persist"—the Church in the United States will be the loser. Further erosion of the authority of the pope and the bishops will be the first and most obvious result. Further erosion of the faith in the hearts of the Catholic faithful will be the ultimate and most damaging result.

Chapter II

What Led to the Catechism for the Universal Church

I.

According to Father Thomas J. Reese, S.J., of the Woodstock Theological Center, the Catechism for the Universal Church currently in preparation under the supervision of a special commission of bishops will, when it is finally issued in 1992 or some time thereafter, be "the most important document to come out of the Vatican since Vatican II". This may very well be true, and, if so, it is significant that Father Reese should be the one to say it, considering that he believes that the provisional text sent out to the Catholic bishops of the world for consultation at the end of 1989 needed at a minimum to be "totally rewritten". More than that, for him, "it is questionable whether a universal catechism is needed at all".[1]

Thus, there does not seem to be any great mystery about why he and his colleagues went to such extraordinary lengths with a symposium, press conference, articles, a book, and so on, if not to derail the Catechism project—he and his colleagues probably realized that they could not quite manage that—at least to compromise and discredit it in advance in the eyes of as many Catholics as they could reach, either directly or via media reports. If a Church teaching is not validly promulgated until it is received [!!], the obvious strategy for this group to follow was to do everything

[1] Quoted in the *National Catholic Reporter,* January 12, 1990. Father Reese repeated this sentiment in the book he subsequently edited composed of symposium contributions: *The Universal Catechism Reader: Reflections and Responses* (San Francisco: Harper Row, 1990), p. 1.

possible to make it likely that this Catechism will simply not be received by the Catholic people. Both Vatican I and Vatican II, though, specifically excluded the notion that the teachings of the pope and bishops require the "consent" of the Church in order to be valid (*Lumen Gentium,* no. 25; *Pastor Aeternus,* no. 4).

The reason why those who hold a different view of the Catholic faith than the Church herself does are so opposed to a catechism in particular was once pungently expressed by Monsignor George A. Kelly, as follows: "The great cop-out of this era is not to answer questions at all. This explains the great decline of catechisms. They provide answers which some of us do not like."[2] Once the Catechism for the Universal Church is finally in place and official, it will never be quite so easy for freewheeling theologians and scholars to "freewheel" again, if such a verb may be permitted.

And not just theologians and scholars either: catechists and teachers of religion at every level in the Church will necessarily be held to stricter account in what they are teaching, once there is an overall standard, or "point of reference". For it is only too true that catechesis, or the teaching of the faith, has been seriously affected by the unprecedented dissent that has been evident in the Church over the past quarter century, especially since the encyclical *Humanae Vitae.* This era has also been characterized by unprecedented confusion in both the manner and the matter of teaching the faith.

This does not mean that there have been no real advances in catechesis in the past quarter century. There have been. Unfortunately though, religious education too often has been compromised, as too often theology has been compromised over the same period, by fashionable importations from "the world"; these importations have not always been compatible with the authentic Catholic faith as handed down. A subsequent chapter will look

[2] Monsignor George A. Kelly, *Who Should Run the Catholic Church? Social Scientists, Theologians, or Bishops?* (Huntington, Ind.: Our Sunday Visitor, 1976), p. 167.

further at this problem and, especially, will survey official Church efforts to remedy the perceived deficiencies in the teaching of religion, efforts that were eventually to lead to the proposal for a Catechism for the Universal Church. At this point, however, it will be sufficient simply to take note of the fact that the problem has existed and persisted, as verified for example, by the 1977 Synod of Bishops, devoted to the subject of catechesis. In the apostolic exhortation *Catechesi Tradendae* that came out of that Synod two years later, Pope John Paul II pointed out that "the Synod fathers realistically recognized, not only an undeniable advance in the vitality of catechetical activity and promising initiatives, but also limitations and even 'deficiencies' in what has been achieved to date". These "limitations", the pope emphasized, "are particularly serious when they endanger integrity of content". On this vital topic of catechetical "content", Pope John Paul II went on to say in *Catechesi Tradendae,*

> the person who becomes a disciple of Christ has the right to receive "the word of faith" not in mutilated, falsified or diminished form, but whole and entire, in all its rigor and vigor. Unfaithfulness on some point to the integrity of the message means a dangerous weakening of catechesis and putting at risk results that Christ and the ecclesial community have a right to expect from it.

In this regard, the Holy Father declared later on in the document, the modern catechetical movement had unfortunately

> brought with it articles and publications which are ambiguous and harmful to young people and to the life of the Church . . . and catechetical works which bewilder the young and even adults, either by deliberately or unconsciously omitting elements essential to the Church's faith, or by attributing excessive importance to certain themes at the expense of others, or, chiefly, by a rather horizontalist overall view out of keeping with the teaching of the Church's magisterium.[3]

[3] Pope John Paul II, Apostolic Exhortation *Catechesi Tradendae* on Catechesis in Our Time, October 16, 1979, nos. 17, 30, and 49.

If this kind of thing has too often characterized the situation of catechesis in the postconciliar Church—and the Holy Father's plain words are pretty definite about that—then one of the primary reasons for the situation in question is the fact that, in the words of one of the postconciliar catechetical experts most often in view, "the catechetical movement over the past fifty years or so has had a symbiotic relationship with biblical scholarship, the liturgical movement, and 'the new theology'."[4] Thus Father Berard Marthaler. Because of the symbiotic relationship he identifies, the catechetical movement has therefore shared some of the mistakes and defects of, and has taken some of the same wrong turns as, "biblical scholarship, the liturgical movement, and 'the new theology' ". Some of these mistakes, defects, and wrong turns leap to the eye, as a matter of fact, as was seen in the positions of some of the contributors to *The Universal Catechism Reader;* more of them will be manifest in the course of the present and the following chapter.

In this second chapter, the principal aim will be, first, to examine the status of catechesis on the eve of the Second Vatican Council, and then to trace, in general terms, how the modern catechetical movement developed. This movement actually began well before the Council; its fruits, though, such as they were, chiefly became evident in the immediate postconciliar era and thus seemed to be as integral to the Council and many of the other changes registered in the Church during the same general period as if the movement had been launched by the Council.

The developments in the catechetical movement to be covered in this chapter will include both the development of the theoretical basis of the new way of teaching religion that emerged and the parallel drive for what may be termed the "professionalization" of Catholic religious education. Finally, the results of these developments in the catechetical movement must be outlined, for it was the consistently poor results of postconciliar catechesis that led to

[4] Father Berard L. Marthaler, "Introduction" to *Sourcebook for Modern Catechetics,* Michael Warren ed. (Winona, Minn.: St. Mary's Press, 1983), p. 19.

the continuing interventions of Church authority to try to remedy what was perceived as a bad situation. This will be chronicled in the next chapter. Eventually, it was these same consistently poor results in transmitting the faith that led to the call for a Catechism for the Universal Church.

2.

It has already been noted that during the first five hundred years of the Church's history formal catechesis generally consisted of oral explanations of the tenets, or "content", of the faith, that is, of the Creed. During the next thousand years within European Christendom, when almost everybody was a member of the Church, catechesis became focused more on the children born into Catholic homes. Still, instruction continued to be given orally for the most part. Catechisms proper only came in with the invention of printing. The Catechism of the Council of Trent was published in 1566 following the conclusion of that ecumenical council, and, virtually down to the nineteen fifties and the eve of Vatican II, the Catholic faith was taught in various countries by means of various national catechisms more or less based on the Roman model, such as the Penny Catechism in Great Britain, the Baltimore Catechism in the United States, and the Italian national Catechism that was updated and made more universal in this century by order of Pope Saint Pius X.[5]

Although these catechisms were all heavily oriented toward imparting the intellectual content of the faith, they were generally used—and it was assumed that they would generally be used—in conjunction with regular and active participation in the sacramental and liturgical life of the Church on the part of those being catechized. So it is not true that these catechisms were nothing more than arid, abstract, lifeless summaries of doctrinal formulas

[5] See Monsignor Eugene Kevane, *Creed and Catechetics: A Catechetical Commentary on the Creed of the People of God* (Westminster, Md.: Christian Classics, 1975), pp. 257–58.

with no reference or relevance to the life of the person being catechized. Indeed, if one judges by how well the typical products of the typical Tridentine catechesis knew and practiced their Catholic faith, especially by comparison with how the typical products of today's new catechesis know and practice theirs, many more favorable things can surely be said about the catechisms of the era than have generally been said in recent years. As Monsignor George A. Kelly, once again, has observed: "If the business of the Church is to bring people into its kingdom, keep them there, and when they wander, get them back, the Tridentine Church was a brilliant success."[6]

Nevertheless religious educators were not happy. The modern catechetical movement grew up in too large a part out of what had become an almost all-pervasive sense of dissatisfaction with the way religion was taught in Catholic schools and Confraternity of Christian Doctrine (CCD) classes in the immediate preconciliar years. To some degree this dissatisfaction extended far beyond the question of catechesis alone and included dissatisfaction with the way Catholics understood and lived their faith generally and with the way the Church was in those days. Catholics in those days supposedly lived in "ghettos" and possessed a narrow "siege mentality" fearful of attack from the modern world or contamination by it. Supposedly too Catholics were concerned only to transmit their own "truths" and "values" within the Church, oblivious to the larger world outside. Moreover, these very Catholic truths and values came more and more under scrutiny and even suspicion by the newly educated kinds of Catholics who, more and more, were also the kinds of Catholics to be found in the ranks of the religious educators. Previously the Church and her beliefs and practices had been scorned and attacked primarily by bigots from outside the Church; suddenly all these things came under attack by the newly sophisticated within the Church who compared the Church with the world outside and too often found her sadly

[6] Kelly, *Who Should Run the Catholic Church?*, p. 57.

wanting. Pope John XXIII's calling of a council to "update" the Church was exactly what these Catholics had been waiting for; they knew exactly in what respects the Church needed to be updated, and it usually turned out to be in almost anything that was "traditional".

A typical popular book of the period, attempting to promote new attitudes that would bring Catholics out of their ghettos, help dissipate their siege mentalities, and move them out into the mainstream of the modern world, was Mary Perkins Ryan's *Are Parochial Schools the Answer?*[7] This book made quite a splash, especially among Catholic educators, when it was published in 1964, while the Council was still going on. The stated purpose of the book was to question the necessity of a separate system of Catholic schools. Such a separate system had grown up because the Catholic bishops of an earlier generation had believed it necessary in Protestant America if the Catholic faith was to be properly preserved and transmitted; in the second half of the nineteenth century, the Catholic bishops had seen American culture as hostile to and subversive of Catholic faith and values. Since the Third Plenary Council of Baltimore in 1884, Catholic pastors had been required to establish schools adjoined to their parishes, and Catholic parents had been required to send their children to these same schools. The long-standing and well-known preconciliar policy of the Catholic Church in this country had thus been established: insofar as possible, Catholic children should be in Catholic schools.

The policy of Catholic children in Catholic classrooms looked at the time as if it would be established forever. The 1917 Code of Canon Law, for example, required bishops to establish schools and also required parents to have permission from their bishop if their children were not in one of these Catholic schools; parents were frequently reminded from the pulpit of their obligations in this regard. By contrast, the 1983 Code of Canon Law merely

[7] Mary Perkins Ryan, *Are Parochial Schools the Answer? Catholic Schools in the Light of the Council* (New York: Holt, Rinehart, and Winston, 1964).

requires pastors of souls to arrange things so that the faithful "may" enjoy a Catholic education.[8]

The Mary Perkins Ryan book introduced quite a number of novel ideas into this environment where it was taken for granted that getting a Catholic education was the normal and natural way for the faith to be passed on to the next generation. Among the Ryan ideas was the idea that what the Catholic schools provided was mostly "emotional security" for Catholics desirous of seeing their children brought up as they had been brought up. Active hostility to the Church on the part of Protestants, Jews, or secularists was seen by Ryan as "a thing of the past".[9] At that time, of course, abortion had not yet been legalized so as to reveal the depths of the continuing hostility to the Church in mainstream America as a result of the Church's unwillingness to condone the killing of children by abortion as the *ne plus ultra* of women's rights.

Catholics of the Ryan type saw no problem with secular society apparently. The problem was with Catholics themselves; they evidently were as "un-American" as their declared enemies had earlier proclaimed them to be. But now the accusations against them under this heading were coming from other Catholics within the Church. Students in Catholic schools and religion classes came to be seen as captive audiences being indoctrinated in religious practices all too typical of those of their mediocre elders; drastic changes were going to be needed as a result of

> ... the fact that so many young Catholics seem bored with religion and cynical about the priestly or religious life; or that so many Catholics hold laissez-faire economic ideas condemned by the Church and right-wing social doctrines completely at odds with papal teaching; or that so many are uninterested in the problem of racial injustice, in society's caring for its sick and aged, in the desperate plight of people in other parts of the world; or that there is a continual leakage from the Church. ...[10]

[8] See Father Harold A. Buetow, *The Catholic School: Its Roots, Identity, and Future* (New York: Crossroad, 1988), p. 169.

[9] Ryan, *Are Parochial Schools the Answer?*, pp. 39–40.

[10] Ibid., p. 47.

It will be noted that this particular litany of criticisms was still situated well within the bounds of Catholic orthodoxy; appeals were included to papal teachings. But within a few short years this author did become an overt dissenter from papal teachings, along with many, many others.[11] Why? As far as one can see, at least in part because her attitude as evidenced by the above quotations (and others in her book) was already fatally tainted by an admixture of condescension toward and even active dislike of average Catholics and their ways and practices—and also with a very American sense of self-sufficiency. For this kind of Catholic the old attitude toward humility and grace no longer sufficed; this kind of Catholic was determined to do better than the old peasant Church of the immigrants. This kind of attitude was no doubt never articulated quite that plainly, but it existed and exists.

Also, although "papal teaching" was invoked, secular standards of justice and caring for the downtrodden were coming to prevail; secular liberal solutions were coming to be seen as vastly superior to the Church's version of social justice; this will be seen to be very pronounced in the catechetical movement later on. But it is already the case that the Church and Catholics were the ones to be judged by secular liberal standards; it was no longer a case of the Church judging the world; that notion seems outlandish to many modern Catholics. But the truth is, of course, that both Catholic social teaching and the typical practice of Catholics, before and after this particular period, were always considerably better in all of these matters than they are usually ever given any credit for being. The kind of secularizing Catholic, however, that was going to turn out to be a very typical feature of the catechetical movement was usually much too impatient with things as they were ever to grant that.

Mary Perkins Ryan, for example, faulted the Church of the day

[11] See Mary Perkins Ryan and John Julian Ryan, "Have You Thought It Out All the Way?", in Daniel Callahan, ed., *The Catholic Case for Contraception* (London: Collier-Macmillan, 1969).

for not believing anything could be done about the basic problems she thought she had identified: nothing could be done

> . . . except to keep working hard and devotedly along the same lines as in the past: providing Mass and the sacraments as conveniently as possible; encouraging devotions old and new, along with spiritual "refreshers" in the form of retreats and missions; inveighing against immoral modern practices such as birth control and indecent dress; and fostering the Catholic school system as the very heart of the Church's endeavor to keep its children true to the faith in the dangerous maelstrom of modern life.[12]

All this was obviously pretty tame and perhaps even boring stuff for the sophisticated new college-educated Catholics who thought they were going to be able to change the world by changing the Church. In point of fact, though, a catechetical movement developing in a climate of such hostility to ordinary Catholics and even to the Church herself was not likely to turn out to be an authentic instrument for the renewal of the Church as called for by Vatican II; the Council issued, after all, a "universal call to holiness", and for those determined to change the world, this could only be more of the same tame and boring stuff.

In spite of many positive achievements, in fact, it remains true that the catechetical movement started out at a great disadvantage as far as fostering any authentic renewal was concerned. Many of those in the catechetical movement soon came to see it as trying to foster justice in the world in secular terms rather than as being responsible for handing on the tenets of an ancient faith; they really did think they were going to change the world by trying to move the Church in directions favored by modern liberal utopianism. Clearly, the old catechism classes were hardly calculated to do that!

This basically negative attitude toward the kind of catechesis that had served the Church for four hundred years was also to be found in sources much more intellectually serious than *Are Paro-*

[12] Ryan, *Are Parochial Schools the Answer?*, p. 47.

chial Schools the Answer?. It was to be found, for example, in the writings of Father Josef A. Jungmann, S.J., the man who was the legitimate father of many of the best results produced by the modern catechetical movement and who otherwise made an immense contribution to the modern Church, for example in his work on the liturgical renewal. With regard to the traditional way of teaching the faith, though, Father Jungmann was able to write about what he called "the frightful ignorance of religion of the masses". He further opined:

> . . . what is lacking among the faithful is a sense of unity, seeing it all as a whole, an understanding of the wonderful message of divine grace. All they retain of Christian doctrine is a string of dogmas and moral precepts, threats and promises, customs and rites, tasks and duties imposed on unfortunate Catholics, whilst the non-Catholic gets off free. They are averse to believing in and acting up to their beliefs, a reluctance which, in an atmosphere of unbelief and materialism, soon leads to disaster for the individual Catholic.
>
> That is how most of us look at the present state of religious ignorance, and that is what we have to face up to. Both our teaching and our catechisms are too much in the nature of theological treatises.[13]

There is, of course, a lot of truth in what Father Jungmann wrote here. In the context of the present discussion, however, it is notable how impatient and exasperated he shows himself to be toward average Christian believers—sinners redeemed by Christ; notable also is a certain arrogance concerning the role that the teacher is supposedly going to play in remedying the deplorable situation he sees, as if he were Pygmalion and those of Christ's little ones given into his hands for formation in the faith were so many statues of his own fashioning. Then there is the judgment that catechisms are just too much like "theological treatises", as if systematic knowledge of the faith were somehow the thing that

[13] Father Josef A. Jungmann, S.J., "Theology and Kerygmatic Teaching", in *Lumen Vitae* 3 (1948): 514, included in Warren, ed., *Sourcebook*, p. 213.

prevented people from being better Christians; that often came to seem the attitude of the catechetical movement, as did Father Jungmann's "I know best" attitude. The catechetical movement was to maintain this latter attitude in the face of all the empirical evidence that the new catechesis did not work. This attitude was even maintained against all the efforts of the hierarchy to try to remedy the situation that will be chronicled in the next chapter.

Another pioneer of the catechetical movement, Father Gerard S. Sloyan, in his well-known and influential book *Shaping the Christian Message,* wrote in a similar vein when he characterized what he called "textbook catechetics" as "orderly, exhaustive, removed from the spirit of Christ's preaching, slightly repellent to the youthful mind".[14] The literature of the catechetical movement abounds in these kinds of critical and negative references to cognitive learning and the Church's traditional ways of handing on the faith, as well as upon the poor quality of the faith and practice of those who were the typical products of this kind of teaching. One would almost think there had never been any Catholics in history who knew and lived and acted upon their faith (whereas the testimony of history, of course, is exactly the opposite of that).

Another "name" in the catechetical movement, Michael Warren, was still able to write even quite recently that "for the Catholic masses, fish on Friday was potentially more important than concern for the poor. The understanding of many persons was a mishmash that could best be accepted in teeth-gritted faith."[15] Yet another such name, Father Berard Marthaler, already quoted above on "the symbiotic relationship" between the new catechesis and some of the other new emphases in the Church and himself a contributor to *The Universal Catechism Reader,* was similarly able to write that "more is required of Christian education than the

[14] Father Gerard S. Sloyan, "Religious Education: From Early Christianity to Medieval Times", in ibid., p. 127.

[15] Michael Warren, Introduction to the chapter on "The Modern Catechetical Movement", in ibid., p. 193.

handing on of shopworn formulas, tired customs, and trite devotions".[16]

"Shopworn formulas, tired customs, and trite devotions": such was the view of Catholics and of the Church that prevailed in the catechetical movement. This all-pervasive air of discontent or dissatisfaction was not limited merely to deploring how poorly the faith had been taught in the past and how mediocre the products of this kind of teaching were; it extended to how the faith should be taught to the upcoming generation, and this was generally interpreted to mean: certainly *not* the way it had been taught in the past; whatever else might be done there certainly could not be "doctrine" taught out of a "catechism". Almost overnight it became part of the received wisdom that the present generation could not be taught the old message by the old methods. "Teachers realize that today's adolescents will not accept canned truths", declared one very influential text used for training catechists and teachers. "One cannot 'teach them religion' in the sense of inculcating any kind of Catholic ready answers."[17]

If one reflects for a moment upon this last statement, it will be seen to be really a pretty drastic one; it amounts to saying before the task is even attempted that catechists cannot in the nature of the case carry out the task that is assigned to them, namely, teaching the faith to the next generation. Unfortunately, it became an all-too-typical attitude in the catechetical movement as well as being, as could have been predicted, a self-fulfilling prophecy.

Yet another popular and influential book repeated the same litany: "Gusty winds of cultural change and religious freedom have blown into the buildings devoted to Catholic education", wrote the authors of *We Were Never Their Age* in 1972. "This has forced religion teachers to re-examine their methods in order to communicate with a broad spectrum of students. . . . The religion teacher can no longer be the authority figure who informs young

[16] Father Berard Marthaler, "The Modern Catechetical Movement in Roman Catholicism: Issues and Personalities", in ibid., p. 278.

[17] Mary Perkins Ryan, ed., *Helping Adolescents Grow up in Christ* (New York: Paulist Press/Deus Books, 1967), Foreword.

people what they as baptized Catholics must be and do under pain of being read out of the club. . . . Religious educators are saying it again and again: the basic problem of kids is not becoming Christian but becoming human."[18] In other words, the Christian message itself that religious educators are supposed to be handing on as their primary task no longer has any importance, but rather, simply "becoming human" is what is important.

Once religious educators have come to think in this fashion, the only conclusion that they or anybody else could logically reach is that, indeed, they really do not have much, if anything, to pass on; and once that point has been reached, as it very quickly was reached by the catechetical movement, the door was open to the doctrineless, noncognitive, "experiential" kind of catechesis that in fact emerged and so bewildered almost everybody who encountered it because most people did not understand where the religious educators were coming from. It seemed pretty clear that what the new catechesis was purveying had certainly not originated from the treasure house of the Church's deposit of faith; but beyond that it was mostly mystifying how the new catechesis could be represented as training or formation in the Catholic faith at all.

A messenger who has come to disbelieve and even scorn his own message is not likely to be very effective or persuasive. And so it has been with the modern catechetical movement; it almost necessarily ended up with the vapid "attitudinizing" and "experiencing" that became its hallmarks once it no longer saw itself as handing on a definite message—one with specific content—the message of the apostles of Jesus that had been handed down, generation after generation, in the Church.

3.

The modern catechetical movement, since it began with such a critical evaluation of earlier catechesis and then itself ended up

[18] James D. DiGiacomo and Edward Wakin, *We Were Never Their Age* (New York: Holt, Rinehart, and Winston, 1972), pp. 154–55.

being almost devoid of a concrete Christian message to pass on, might at first seem to have contributed little or nothing at all to the Church's perennial task of handing on the faith she has from Christ.

Actually, in the beginning, this was not so. In the hands of such pioneers as Father Josef Jungmann and Father Johannes Hofinger, both Austrian Jesuits, the modern catechetical movement began as a worthy and serious effort to return to the sources of Christianity and to try to proclaim anew the good news of salvation in Jesus Christ; it aimed to do this in a way, hopefully, not dissimilar to the way in which the Gospel had originally been preached. At this stage in its development, the catechetical movement focused on the *kerygma,* or proclamation of the good news, as has already been mentioned in the last chapter; and thus it was also called, for a short time, "the kerygmatic movement" as often as it was called the catechetical movement in those days.

As its name implied, the kerygmatic movement still very much aimed at imparting a message; it still focused on content. Its chief aim was nothing else but "to present the truth of our faith as an organic whole. Its core [was] the good news of our redemption in Christ. Its fruit [was to] be the grateful response of our love."[19] In order to evoke this response of love, it concentrated on a *person:* Jesus Christ; it was therefore what came to be called "Christocentric". To achieve all its aims, it laid great emphasis upon the use of both Scripture and liturgy in catechesis; but it also insisted upon what was called "systematic teaching", including adequate textbooks, and "the testimony of Christian living". Indeed, liturgy, Scripture, systematic teaching, and the example of Christian living quickly became enshrined as a "fourfold presentation of the faith" that was one of the principal characteristics of the kerygmatic movement.[20]

An excellent summary of the aims and methods of the kerygmatic

[19] "General Conclusions of the Eichstätt Study Week", in Warren, ed., *Sourcebook,* p. 30.

[20] "Basic Principles of Modern Catechetics: A Summary Report from Eichstätt", in ibid., p. 35.

approach to catechesis is the following from the *Sourcebook for Modern Catechetics* edited by Michael Warren:

> —Since the history of salvation is recounted in the Bible, catechetics must use a *biblical language.*
>
> —Since the salvation portrayed in the Bible finds its active outlet in the liturgy, catechetics must use *liturgical language.*
>
> —Since this redeeming work of God is seen day after day in the life of the Church and of each of its members, the "testimony" must shine through catechetics as an *existential language.*
>
> —Since this history of salvation, narrated in the Bible, celebrated in the liturgy, and experienced in everyday life, takes a progressively concrete form in the shape of the Church, catechetics must use as well the *doctrinal language.* [21]

Far from there being anything wrong with this, these fundamental principles of the kerygmatic approach were seen to constitute a definite contribution to the teaching of religion; if the catechetical movement had stayed on this road, all would have been well. Indeed, some of these kerygmatic principles were warmly embraced and adopted by the magisterium of the Church. Thus, Pope John Paul II wrote as follows in *Catechesi Tradendae:* "Through catechesis the Gospel *kerygma* (the initial ardent proclamation by which a person is one day overwhelmed and brought to the decision to entrust himself to Jesus Christ by faith) is gradually deepened, developed in its implicit consequences, explained in language that includes an appeal to reason, and channeled towards Christian practice in the Church and the world."[22]

There is a very real sense, in other words, in which the kerygmatic approach to handing on the faith is even rather an ideal method. Pope John Paul II was actually to stress, as the kerygmatic movement did too at its beginnings, what he called "the Christocentricity of all authentic catechesis". This was, again, in *Catechesi Tradendae;* and the Pope went on to declare that "at

[21] Luis Erdozain, "The Evolution of Catechetics: A Survey of Six International Study Weeks on Catechetics", in ibid., p. 90.

[22] John Paul II, *Catechesi Tradendae.*

the heart of catechesis, we find, in essence, a person, the Person of Jesus of Nazareth".[23] Earlier, the *General Catechetical Directory* had also stressed the necessary Christocentricity of all catechesis and had also stressed as elementary that "catechesis . . . demands the witness of faith".[24]

Thus, the kerygmatic approach was in its beginnings a distinct asset for religious education in the Catholic Church, and it was to be clearly recognized as such by the Church's magisterium. Nevertheless, as has already been noted above, it remains true that one of the principal motivations for the new approach was Father Jungmann's apparent conviction that all the catechesis that had come before him was lamentably deficient. Apparently the Church had not really been able to teach her faith properly since the earliest centuries. "Jungmann put more emphasis on the need for a religious understanding of the Christian message than on orthodox interpretation of certain doctrines and proper teaching methods", Father Marthaler has observed. "The *kerygma* is 'good news' which should be welcomed, not looked upon as imposing a fabric of joyless obligations."[25] If it is true that Jungmann thus looked upon the catechesis previous to him in this fashion, namely as "a fabric of joyless obligations" imposed upon unwilling subjects, then this was an assumption deserving of much more of the scholarly thoroughness for which Jungmann was famous, rather than simply being taken for granted as, too often, it was taken for granted by the catechetical movement. When to this critical attitude about the Church's customary catechesis there was added a disdain for the "orthodox interpretation of certain doctrines and proper teaching methods", then the formula was already present for the catechetical movement to go astray, as was, in the end, to be the case.

It is possible to trace how the catechetical movement's gradual

[23] Ibid., no. 5.

[24] Sacred Congregation for the Clergy, *General Catechetical Directory* (Washington, D.C.: United States Catholic Conference Publications Office, 1971), nos. 35, 40.

[25] Marthaler, "Modern Catechetical Movement".

loss of interest in the content of the faith—the Christian message itself—came about. The quickest and easiest way to do this is to look at the results of a number of the International Catechetical Study Weeks that were prominent features on the catechetical scene in the 1960s and had an enormous influence on the direction taken by the catechetical movement and on its own self-understanding. One of the principal stated purposes of these International Catechetical Study Weeks was to examine the teaching of the faith in the light of the needs of the missions, but they ended up influencing the accepted "state of the art" in the teaching of religion generally. These conferences were attended by catechetical theorists, theologians, and other experts, and what they came up with had an effect. The first of the conferences was organized, as were the subsequent ones, by Father Johannes Hofinger, S.J., who had already assumed the Jungmann mantle. This first Catechetical Study Week was held at Nijmegen, the Netherlands, in 1959, and examined the relationship between catechesis and the liturgy.

Perhaps the most important of all these International Study Weeks was held in Eichstätt, Germany, in 1960. This was the conference *par excellence* devoted to the kerygmatic movement. It established the aims and principles of the whole kerygmatic approach, introduced its fourfold presentation of the faith through liturgy, Bible, systematic teaching, and the example of Christian living, and called for further development and study along the same lines. It would be difficult to exaggerate the importance of this Eichstätt conference; an important part of what it accomplished has been officially adopted by the Church's magisterium. Had the catechetical movement continued on the trail blazed by this particular International Catechetical Study Week, its end results might have turned out to be very different from what they in fact turned out to be.

The third International Catechetical Study Week held in 1962 in Bangkok, Thailand, introduced the then novel notion of "pre-evangelization", whereby it was seen as the task of catechesis not only to present the faith but "to prepare the ground by purifying judgments, sentiments, and even subconscious impressions to lead them to a fuller response to the doctrine of Christ . . . and to lay special emphasis on adaptation by developing the doctrine according to analogies, images, or forms of expression familiar to people of a given region or culture".[26] Here again, the catechetical task was still seen as in some sense conveying "the doctrine of Christ", even though the notion of "adapting" the faith introduced a possibly troublesome new element. It cannot be repeated too often that the faith is something that was "delivered once for all to the saints" (Jude 3) and has never in the Church's tradition been considered something to be adapted but rather something to be handed down intact. However that may be, as originally formulated, the whole notion of pre-evangelization certainly fell within an orthodox framework and has, again, since been accepted by the Church's magisterium; it was incorporated, for example, into Pope Paul VI's apostolic exhortation *Evangelii Nuntiandi* in 1975.[27] (The term itself evidently originated in the work of the French Dominican, Father Pierre-André Liégé, work actually carried out prior to Vatican II.)[28]

At the Pan-African Catechetical Study Week at Katigondo in 1964 and that at Manila, the Philippines, in 1967, the telltale corrosive criticisms of the Church as she actually is made their appearances. Vatican II had drawn to its end, and then was over, and the atmosphere was definitely changing rapidly. Katigondo found it necessary to "warn against the wrong use of the scholastic method",[29] while Manila felt obliged to trot out the whole by now familiar panoply of a Church "glaringly foreign in her way of life, her liturgy, architecture, and even her mentality . . . a ghetto group that seemed more concerned with the defense of its privileges than the building up of the human community . . . little

[26] Alfonso Nebreda, "East Asian Study Week on Mission Catechetics: 1962", in Warren, ed., *Sourcebook,* p. 45.

[27] Pope Paul VI, Apostolic Exhortation *Evangelii Nuntiandi* on Evangelization in the Modern World, December 8, 1975, no. 51.

[28] Erdozain, "Evolution of Catechetics", p. 93.

[29] "Final Resolutions: Pan-African Catechetical Week: Katigondo, 1964", in Warren, ed., *Sourcebook,* p. 55.

committ[ed] to social reform and to the struggle for social justice".[30] This "struggle for social justice" would soon far outweigh in importance any such thing as a "doctrine of the faith" in the minds of many catechetical theorists; this kind of attitude was at the heart of what would later come to be called "liberation theology".

One of the reasons religious education has gotten off the track generally in the postconciliar era is that it has too often gotten sidetracked into things that, however important in themselves, are not in fact the primary aim of catechesis. Social justice, for example, is very important, and it is very important for the Church too, as evidenced by the considerable body of her social teachings at both the papal and episcopal levels. Moreover, the Church possesses an excellent record on most social justice issues. But social justice, as such, is not the point of catechesis but rather the whole content of the faith is.

By the time the sixth of the International Catechetical Study Weeks came about, in Medellín, Colombia, in 1968, the thrust to change the world by means of the new catechesis rather than (so much more modestly) merely being content to focus on trying to hand on the faith effectively was long since in full swing. And thus "Christocentrism" was virtually lost in the shuffle, while the struggle to render man autonomous and free and to fight exploitation and injustice came to the fore. As the eleventh of the General Conclusions of the conference at Medellín phrased it:

> Catechetics today, in accordance with a more adequate theology of Revelation [!!], realizes that the first place to look when seeking God's design for contemporary man is the area of history and authentically human aspirations. These are an *indispensable part* of the contents of catechetics [emphasis in the original].[31]

"*The first place to look* [emphasis added] when seeking God's design . . . is the area of history and authentically human aspira-

[30] "The Implications of Vatican II for the Mission in Asia: Manila, 1967", in ibid., pp. 58, 63.

[31] Erdozain, "Evolution of Catechetics", p. 101.

tions. . . . " Not in Scripture, not in Tradition, not in the guidance afforded by the living magisterium of the Church, but in contemporary history!

This is surely the same basic mentality already encountered above to the effect that "the basic problem of kids is not becoming Christian but becoming human".[32] At the end of a decade of intensive activity and development within the catechetical movement, the theorists and experts finally discovered that the *indispensable* element of catechesis comes not from Christ and his revelation handed down in the Church but from the human, all-too-human "area of history and authentically human aspirations". This is "liberation theology" with a vengeance. How has it come to be the basis of the teaching of religion? What is going on here? These are questions any Catholic who still believes the faith would have a right to ask; the wonder is that more of them have not asked what the state of the art in religious education in their Church has been allowed to become. The very people charged with the task of finding better and more effective ways of handing on the faith unilaterally decide that what is important is not handing on the faith at all but rather the struggle for social justice, and many do not even notice!

What is really going on when professional teachers of religion are suddenly found declaring that it is not what is "Christian" that is important but what is "human"? What is really going on when the acknowledged and recognized theorists and experts on the subject of handing on the tenets of a revealed religion are similarly found declaring that it is what is "revealed" by "history" and "human aspirations" that is the important thing? (This is not the last time, by the way, that such a notion of "revelation" will be encountered in the course of this study.)

Strange as all this may seem when stated so baldly, it is exactly what a study of the documents pertaining to the six International Catechetical Study Weeks yields. A perusal of some of the modern theoretical books and articles on catechesis yields the same evidence. The wonder of it all, again, is how little the whole shift has been

[32] DiGiacomo and Wakin, *We Were Never Their Age.*

noted. Yet it was in no way an arbitrary or overnight transformation; there was a logic and a progression behind it, some of which has already been glimpsed in the course of this study. Basically what occurred in catechesis was a shift from God to man; from supernatural faith to more human concerns; from proclaiming the good news of salvation in Jesus Christ and everything that follows from that to espousing a purely human kind of effort featuring a struggling humanity trying to save itself by political means from oppression and injustice.

In terms of the six International Catechetical Study Weeks that have been briefly reviewed here, the key development that marked the shift from concentrating on the divine to concentrating on the human came at the 1962 conference in Bangkok. At this conference, the kerygmatic method with its emphasis on the original message of Christ was still supposedly accepted by the catechetical theorists present. However, with the adoption of the necessity for the psychological and sociological preconditioning for the acceptance of the faith inherent in the concept of pre-evangelization, another new element was introduced. In itself, as has already been pointed out, the concept of pre-evangelization is compatible with the faith and acceptable to the Church; properly understood, it has been fruitful for catechesis.

However, the way in which the Bangkok conference came to understand the idea of pre-evangelization, followed by the way the catechetical movement in general took up the idea and developed and applied it, truly did introduce a radical new factor into catechesis powerful enough to bring about the shift from concentrating on the divine to concentrating on the human (and therefore no longer concentrating on Christ's revelation of himself as Lord and Savior). For the Bangkok Catechetical Study Week explicitly decided that pre-evangelization had to be "anthropocentric", that is, concentrated, precisely, on the human. "The guiding principle of pre-evangelization is anthropocentric", the conference concluded, "because we must start with man as he is".[33]

[33] Quoted by Erdozain, "Evolution of Catechetics", p. 94.

"Anthropocentric", then. A catechetical writer charting the history of the six International Catechetical Study Weeks candidly described this development, without even a hint of self-criticism or objectivity, as follows: "The balance now is tilting quite decidedly in favor of humankind. The anthropocentric movement takes over from the kerygmatic."[34] This same writer seemed calmly and totally unaware that this new anthropocentric approach represented something revolutionary, something totally different from anything accepted or even imagined in religious education up to that time. This writer did see that the kerygmatic movement and the new anthropocentric movement represented "two completely different attitudes of mind. The kerygmatic attitude refers back constantly to the Bible and the liturgy . . . the anthropological attitude in contrast opts for the psychological approach, renouncing the already acquired treasures [namely, the content of the faith], it seeks its ends choosing insecurity and hardship."[35]

Those who attended these catechetical conferences and were influenced by them were generally quite conscious of the shift that was taking place—the shift away from Christ and his saving faith to the world and its concerns. Talk of this shift away from preoccupation with transmitting a revealed message to getting involved in purely human concerns was in the air in catechetical circles. Books were published on the subject of how the kerygmatic movement, itself such a recent novelty on the catechetical scene, was already becoming passé.[36] The new humanistic emphasis

[34] Ibid.

[35] Ibid., p. 96.

[36] Alfonso Nebreda, *Kerygma in Crisis* (Chicago: Loyola University Press, 1965). Nebreda frankly proposed to "re-situate" religious education by moving it out of its third phase, catechesis, and concentrating on its first phase, pre-evangelization: "I want to make it perfectly clear that the approach in pre-evangelization is different from the approach used in catechesis proper" (pp. 102–3). Catechetical practitioners in general seem to have been quite aware of the radical implications of their shift from "Christocentrism" to "anthropocentrism", namely, that teaching efforts would no longer be focused on teaching the *faith;* in other words, the very nature of the catechetical

soon reached all the way down to the catechists in the parishes. New religion textbooks started to come out reflecting the new emphasis as well, since religion textbook publishers, then as now, generally took their cues from the developing catechetical movement and tried to produce "the latest thing"—vied with each other in trying to produce it, as a matter of fact. Parents, pastors, and teachers who had not been following developments in the catechetical movement were often baffled by the new approach and the new religion books; usually they were assured that all was well, though, and that the catechetical people knew what they were doing. However, most Catholics to this day are simply unaware that there was any catechetical movement behind all of this; and hence the bafflement about the new catechesis often persists to this day.

Those who were following the developing catechetical movement, however, were greatly influenced by the six International Catechetical Study Weeks among other influences that were in the air, and they were generally conscious of the shift from the old "personal salvation" approach to the emphasis on social activism of a leftist variety that was too often coming to take the place of transmitting the faith in religious education. Although quite conscious of the shift, these people seem to have been much less conscious of the meaning and implications of that shift, namely, that concentrating on man and his world and his human concerns, as was now the fashion in religious education, was basically *incompatible* with the task assigned by the Church to catechists and

---

mission became radically altered—almost beyond recognition. See also Didier-Jacques Piveteau, F.S.C., and James T. Dillon, *Resurgence of Religious Education* (Notre Dame, Ind.: Religious Education Press, 1977). These authors point out that "pre-evangelization" arises out of a conception of theology "which separates the things of man from those of God? Explicit reference to Jesus Christ is withheld . . . " (p. 55). How anyone could possibly expect to teach the faith of Jesus Christ without mentioning him is hard to understand, but the point is that what was being abandoned was, precisely, the teaching of the faith of Jesus Christ! Yet nobody seems to have remarked on this at the time as anything out of the ordinary.

religion teachers of transmitting the revealed faith of Christ. Yet nobody seemed to notice the discrepancy particularly; Christ's name often continued to be invoked in words, as it continues to be today in liberation theology. However, the content of religious education had indeed become very different from what it had been when the average parent had studied his or her catechism. Those indoctrinated in the new catechesis, however, saw no conflict or opposition in any of this. The catechetical writer quoted above blissfully wrote that "there is no opposition at all; rather, a progression, the same line of thought taken to greater depth. The anthropological orientation appears... more as the unexpected fruit of the seed sown by the kerygmatic renewal", this writer opined.[37]

Thus, a movement that had been expressly organized in order to find ways to teach more effectively the faith of Christ as it had been handed down in the Church actually developed to a point where it in effect abandoned the teaching of the faith of Christ as its principal task, aiming instead to create a new and supposedly more human world by manipulating the attitudes of Catholic children placed in religion classes for the purpose of learning their faith. Strange as this transformation may seem on reflection, what is said about it here is no exaggeration of what happened to the theoretical basis of catchesis in the modern catechetical movement in the course of the revolutionary 1960s; it can be amply documented in the writings of catechetical theorists; and, of course, it was precisely parallel to the aberrations developing at around the same time in the new theology and the new liturgy. This same era saw the rise of "dissent" from authoritative Catholic teachings, and, in the climate thus created, the new catechesis did not even seem particularly out of place.

The situation of catechesis in the Church since the late 1960s has been marked by more or less continually recurring disputes about what was being taught in religion classes and how it was being taught. The next chapter will chart the recurring efforts of

[37] Erdozain, "Evolution of Catechetics", p. 96.

the Holy See and the bishops to try to restore authentic Catholic doctrine to Catholic religion classes; but most of these disputes and efforts took place at least in partial ignorance of how the catechetical movement had been developing and how subversive of any historical, revealed faith were the conclusions it had arrived at by the mid-1960s. It truly is, of course, hard to understand how a movement founded to improve ways of teaching the faith could wind up after a decade or two deciding that teaching the faith was not even what was important; but then the new Catholic theology followed a path that was disturbingly similar, which is one of the reasons Catholic theologians can be viewed on TV today assuring the world that what the magisterium continues to teach about, say, abortion or sexual morality, is not necessarily the position of "the Church".

Religious educators, for their part, initiated gradually into the developments of the catechetical movement as these emerged, generally went along with these developments and brushed aside any criticisms of them as motivated by the ignorance and obtuseness of those who simply wanted to see their children taught as they themselves had been taught. One of the principal resolutions of the English-speaking group at an International Catechetical Congress held in Rome in the summer of 1971 under the auspices of the Congregation for the Clergy read, for example, as follows:

> Some parent groups and adults are concerned that much of what is being taught in modern religious education programs and through modern religious textbooks is different from what they learned as children. Many even accuse religion teachers and textbook writers of doctrinal error, omissions, or misplaced emphasis. Recognizing the existence of this situation, which in many instances is polarizing the Christian community, this congress should want to reassure these groups about the great and valuable progress made in religious education during the past quarter of a century.[38]

[38] "Final and Approved Resolutions of the English-speaking Language Group", International Catechetical Congress, September 1971, in Warren, ed., *Sourcebook,* p. 82.

It can pretty safely be granted that those "groups" concerned about the authentic character of what religious education had too often become by 1971 were indeed unaware of the particular kind of "progress made in religious education". Nevertheless, as has been noted earlier, Pope John Paul II in *Catechesi Tradendae* was clearly to recognize the problem of "doctrinal error, omissions, or misplaced emphasis" in religious education and to put on the record that it was, unhappily, a fact; it was not simply an illusion of those thinking that religion should always be taught the way it had been taught to them. Religious educators generally declined to admit the existence of any doctrinal error, and, oddly, this point was often conceded to them; nobody in authority ever seemed to want to look at the actual religion books in use to see if there *was* any error in them; the whole issue of possible doctrinal error was usually handled in the polite, bland, and gingerly way that Church authorities have generally used in approaching doctrinal deviations in the postconciliar period. For how could such fine, sincere, and dedicated people as the religious educators ever be "heretics"? Perish the thought! Both the word and the idea were something out of the Middle Ages!

Another resolution from the same 1971 International Catechetical Congress in Rome cited above papered over the real problem in a way that had become almost routine by then:

> We should encourage mutual charity, honest dialogue, and a sincere search for understanding and reconciliation among the varying views within the Catholic community. It must be made clear that, in any age, the truths of the faith always remain the same and the congress would disassociate itself from any deviation from this doctrinal norm. However, the manner in which they are expressed necessarily varies according to cultural, social, and linguistic conditions. In addition, Catholic adults must be helped to realize that Catholic doctrine grows and develops.[39]

The whole debate over doctrinal content in religious education had thus already reached the point where the debaters were

[39] Ibid.

simply talking past one another; it was a true *dialogue des sourds.* The same 1971 International Catechetical Congress in Rome served in other ways to demonstrate how ecclesiastical authority was not really coming to grips with a religious education establishment by then more or less operating autonomously and taking its primary direction from the catechetical movement and from freewheeling theologians and other theorists rather than from the magisterium of the Church.

The *General Catechetical Directory* had just been issued at the time of the International Catechetical Congress, and one of the things the Congress participants succeeded in doing was to wrest a statement from a no doubt reluctant Cardinal John Wright, the prefect of the Congregation for the Clergy, to the effect that the GCD was merely a "service document" promulgating guidelines rather than "legislation" binding upon religious educators. They wanted nothing binding upon them, naturally. "The basic purpose of the Directory", Cardinal Wright ended up declaring at a press conference on June 17, 1971, "is to provide an orientation for religious formation, rather than to establish binding rules."[40]

This was a typical example of a phenomenon that will be more fully described in the next chapter, namely, how professionals and religious educators have regularly converted what formerly would have been automatically understood to be mandates or prescriptions into "service documents" (that do not have to serve), into "directories" (that do not direct in the sense that they need not be followed), and "guidelines" that, in the words of Monsignor William B. Smith, "offer no guidance and draw no lines".[41]

4.

The 1971 International Catechetical Congress in Rome brought out some other issues in contemporary religious education besides

[40] Ibid., p. 81.

[41] *Fellowship of Catholic Scholars Newsletter,* June 1990.

those already mentioned. One of these issues was the defiance exhibited at the parish level toward the restored Church policy, set forth in an appendix to the *General Catechetical Directory,* of providing First Confession for children prior to their First Communion. Another issue concerned the question of whether or not there were two distinct kinds of "revelation" in Catholicism; closely related to this issue was another one concerning the question of whether religion could not most effectively be taught by means of "experience" rather than cognitively, that is, by means of doctrinal formulas addressed to the mind. These were all issues that would recur in the course of the preparation of a *National Catechetical Directory* for the United States, as will be seen in the next chapter.

As for the question of revelation, the final and approved resolutions of the English-speaking language group at the International Catechetical Congress held that there were indeed two views of revelation: one that saw it in terms of revealed truths couched in conceptual terms that had to be communicated to students in situations such as classrooms and another view that saw revelation as the self-communication of God, proceeding from what was called an incarnational point of view. This second view, as would soon become clear, conceived of revelation as something to be actually personally experienced.

The English-speaking language group at the International Catechetical Congress held in Rome in 1971 held that the *General Catechetical Directory,* which had just been issued, supported the view that there were two distinct types of revelation.[42] This contention seems not to have been correct, however. What the GCD says about revelation, that is, the words and deeds by which God revealed himself to humanity in the history of his Chosen People, in their prophets, and, finally, especially in his own son Jesus Christ, is that this "divine revelation, which constitutes the object of the Catholic faith . . . was completed at the time of the apostles". Moreover, always according to the GCD, this divine

[42] "Final and Approved Resolutions", in Warren, ed., *Sourcebook.*

revelation "must be clearly distinguished from the grace of the Holy Spirit, without whose inspiration and illumination no one can believe". The GCD then goes on to say:

> On the other hand, God, who formerly spoke to the human race by revealing himself through divine deeds together with the message of the prophets, of Christ, and of the apostles, even now secretly directs, through the Holy Spirit, in sacred tradition, by the light and sense of the faith, the Church, his bride, and he speaks with her, so that the People of God, under the leadership of the magisterium, may attain a fuller understanding of revelation.[43]

In other words, God, having revealed himself once and for all, went on to confide to his Church the task of interpreting this once-and-for-all revelation of himself; the Catholic faithful must therefore look to the Church in order to understand this revelation and follow it and apply it to the circumstances of their lives. This explanation is hardly an endorsement of any "on-going revelation".

The catechetical movement, however, having arrived at Medellín at the idea that "God's design" is most truly to be discerned in "history and authentically human aspirations", was, perhaps understandably from its own point of view, quite anxious that the whole concept of "revelation" not be confined to what was delivered up to the time of the apostles, henceforth to be authentically interpreted by the magisterium of the Church. The catechetical movement required a concept of revelation that understood God to be continuing to "reveal" himself all the time in human experiences. This may not have been what the GCD actually said, but it was nevertheless quite important to find it present in what the GCD did say about revelation. This was done.

"Though the Christ-event has taken place 'once and for all' at a definite moment of history", declared one of the most influential of the speakers at the 1971 International Catechetical Congress, "still, as far as we are concerned, the revelation of God in Jesus

[43] Sacred Congregation for Clergy, *General Catechetical Directory,* no. 13.

Christ is an on-going process, is an ever-present happening in which each one of us has to be involved, and to which each one of us has to respond and react. It is an on-going process of a growing and widening interpersonal relation[ship]."[44]

"Still, as far as we are concerned . . ." This, of course, is nothing more than a bare assertion, without argument or proof, that "the revelation of God in Jesus Christ is an on-going process". No evidence is offered to support this viewpoint, and it is not what the GCD actually says. To be sure, every believer does participate in an "on-going process of a growing and widening interpersonal relation[ship]" with Jesus Christ the Savior, but this is hardly "divine revelation" in the sense in which the Church understands and has always understood that term. This on-going relationship of the believer with Christ is in any case entirely explainable in terms of the GCD's careful distinction, quoted above, between divine revelation properly speaking, and the grace, inspiration, and illumination of the Holy Spirit, which do assist the believer on an on-going basis.

This would not do, however, as far as the catechetical movement was concerned. For the catechetical movement there had to be an "on-going revelation", and it had to be something experienced by the believer; otherwise, among other problems, how rescue catechesis from the arid, abstract, and shopworn doctrinal formulas and definitions of the past that had come to seem so intolerable to religious educators? Yet it is not at all clear how something can continue to be a matter of "faith" or "belief" if it is in fact actually "experienced".

Once the events or experiences of one's personal life become the basis for a "revelation" or for "faith", then the stage is set to abandon Christianity and its claim of special divine revelation delivered once and for all in history ("He suffered under Pontius Pilate") and handed down through the generations in a living Church. Strange as it may seem, though, adopting "experience" as

[44] D. S. Amalorparadass, "Catechesis as a Pastoral Task of the Church", in Warren, ed., *Sourcebook,* p. 348.

the basis for "revelation" came to be the position adopted by many, perhaps even a majority, of modern Catholic religious educators—certainly those trained in the ideas and notions of the modern catechetical movement. Many of these educators *did* abandon "revelation", as the Church understands it, during the 1960s and 1970s. Thus, one who was considered a leader in the catechetical movement over many years was able to write in 1972: "Were anyone to start looking for a revelation in the events available as events, that is, in the day-to-day experiences of his life, he would have to reject any document from the past pretending to divine revelation"—such as, presumably, the four Gospels.[45]

True. If "revelation" arises out of the events of one's own life, then the events in the life of the first-century Palestinian Jew named Jesus are quite clearly not revealed in the same way; nobody living today has had, or could have had, a personal experience of Jesus preaching to the crowds or eating with his disciples. What the catechetical movement leaves out while getting so preoccupied with personal experiences are, precisely, the "day-to-day experiences" in the lives of the apostles of Jesus who were the witnesses of what occurred and of what was subsequently handed down in the Church; it is their original experience and witness that is the basis of the faith of Christians. The personal experiences of these same Christians are necessarily something else; they may supplement or contribute to faith, but they are not, and cannot be, the basis of faith. What is strange is how any Catholic could imagine that experience could be the basis of faith; yet this became one of the principal tenets of modern Catholic religious educators in the postconciliar era.

Yet it is not actually so strange that some religious educators should have adopted this position, considering what their premises were. On the contrary, it was quite logical. What was strange was that they should have continued to consider themselves Catholic once they had adopted the premises they had adopted.

[45] Gabriel Moran, *The Present Revelation* (New York: Herder and Herder, 1972), p. 33.

Once experience did nevertheless become a major criterion for what was considered the latest thing in catechesis, the descent into a creedless and contentless noncognitive type of catechesis became extremely rapid, just as the shift from the kerygmatic to the anthropocentric approach was very rapid. In fact, the emphasis on personal experience is, psychologically, analogous to the emphasis on the anthropocentric, socially speaking. The shift is analogous in both cases; the catechetical movement has been very logical and consistent in this regard. If "social justice" became the new content of catechesis as a result of the Bangkok International Catechetical Study Week, then "experience" was similarly established by the time of the 1971 International Catechetical Conference in Rome. In fact as early as 1970, the Dutch theologian Piet Schoonenberg was already writing: "From a mere approach to the message, experience has become the theme itself of catechesis. Catechesis has become the interpretation of experience. It has to clarify experience, that is, it has to articulate and enlighten the experience of those for whom the message is intended."[46]

There can be no question that this kind of experiential catechesis represented another shift from the divine to the human, in this case, from Jesus and his truths revealed for the sake of our salvation to the individual and his experiences. Actually, both the anthropocentric and the experiential approaches to catechesis imply that catechesis is henceforth to be *psychological;* psychology is the new basis, not Christ and his message. If any doubt had remained about this, it was made abundantly clear by the kinds of pedagogical approaches promoted by leading catechetical theorists. To "start with the learner", and not, for example, with the content of the message to be conveyed

> . . . is to recognize that learning is a psychological process and not a logical one. It is to recognize that the learner learns according to the rules of his personality and not according to the logical rules of doctrine or of the Bible or of the liturgy. It

[46] Piet Schoonenberg, S.J., "Revelation and Experience", *Lumen Vitae* 25 (1970): 552, in Marthaler, "Modern Catechetical Movement", p. 282.

> is to affirm the indisputable fact that the learner acquires substantive and structural content according to the dynamics of his abilities and needs, and not according to the structure of doctrine or of the Bible or of liturgy.[47]

This is the only way experiential catechesis could have gone, considering its premises; yet it *means,* necessarily, downgrading the message of Christ. It should also be remembered that experiential catechesis has been rather markedly an American thing; presumably it has been seen as congenial to the national pragmatism. Father Berard Marthaler was even able to write, apparently proudly:

> If North Americans have made a distinctive contribution to modern catechetics (and I would argue that we have), it is in this area of experiential catechesis. Experience is a theme which runs through the educational literature of the United States like a haunting melody; some contend it is simply another aspect of American pragmatism. Despite a certain abhorrence among Roman Catholics for John Dewey's philosophy earlier in this century, his influence in contemporary catechetics is as unmistakable as it is pervasive.[48]

It is understandable that the former hostility to Dewey would be dissipated once religious educators had put aside the tenets of a supernatural faith that was precisely what was incompatible with Dewey's pragmatic approach to education.

The truth is, though, that the rash and precipitous descent into experiential catechesis by religious educators in this country was carried out in the face of explicit magisterial warnings to the contrary. "It is . . . not sufficient for catechesis merely to stimulate a religious experience, even if it is a true one", the *General Catechetical Directory* specifies. "Rather, catechesis should contribute to the gradual grasping of the whole truth about the divine plan. . . . "[49]

Similarly, Pope John Paul II, in *Catechesi Tradendae,* teaches

[47] James Michael Lee, *The Religious Education We Need: Toward the Renewal of Christian Education* (Mishawaka, Ind.: Religious Education Press, 1977).

[48] Marthaler, "Modern Catechetical Movement".

[49] Sacred Congregation for Clergy, *General Catechetical Directory,* no. 24.

that "it is quite useless to campaign for the abandonment of serious and orderly study of the message of Christ in the name of a method concentrating on life experience. No one can arrive at the whole truth on the basis solely of some simple private experience, that is to say, without an adequate experience of the message of Christ."[50]

5.

One of the things that has emerged out of this study is the fact that there is today an identifiable group of religious educators, what may be termed a "religious education establishment". This establishment has been formed by the modern catechetical movement; indeed it seems to look consistently for guidance and direction to the catechetical movement and to new theologians allied to it rather than to the magisterium of the Church. It does not overtly oppose the magisterium or defy it; it simply goes on doing its own thing, implementing the ideas of the catechetical movement; and it is able to do this because it enjoys a high degree of autonomy, being charged with carrying out the Church's formal programs of religious education but for the most part simply left to do this on its own.

It is not really too surprising that such a religious education establishment should have grown up and been allowed to operate the way it has. The present age is the age of the expert *par excellence;* nearly everything is turned over to experts of various types, and people commonly disclaim any competence in areas where they do not have any expertise. The Church's task of religious education has similarly and long since been turned over to the people who supposedly know what they are doing, the religious educators—the religious education establishment. The bishops tend to disclaim any direct competence as "experts" in practice; pastors often do the same at the parish level; and this leaves the field free for the religious educators to operate in.

[50] John Paul II, *Catechesi Tradendae,* no. 22.

Whether this typical kind of modern organization to carry out a specific task is really compatible with the Church's mission to transmit her faith or compatible with the fact that the bishops are supposed to be the principal official teachers is another question. The fact is that, in the postconciliar era, the professional religious educators have largely run the educational show. It is for this reason that it is necessary at this point to take a special look at the whole phenomenon of "professionalism" in religious education; it is a peculiarly modern and very widespread phenomenon.

In the heyday of the Catholic school, often favored by pastors over practically any other parish activity and in those days largely staffed by religious sisters, a frequent complaint heard was that these sisters were often not "professionally competent" to teach. Even many lay teachers may have taught in the Catholic schools only because they were not certified or otherwise professionally qualified to hold better-paying positions in the public schools. At times some of this may have been true, although the teaching sisters and other teachers in Catholic schools often made up in other ways for whatever professional qualifications or training they may have lacked, especially in the dedication they so often exhibited in their vocations as teachers, as many products of the Catholic schools of those days will testify. Another thing that was left out in the typical complaint about the lack of professionalism in the Catholic schools was the fact that some of the supposed professional qualifications of school teachers, as established by typical schools or colleges of education in the public sector, were not as a matter of fact often all that substantive or professional anyway, especially by comparison with the solid curricula still often maintained in many Catholic schools descended from traditional European models of a classical education. By and large in America, the public schools operating under the influence of John Dewey and theorists similar to him were steadily becoming denuded of solid curricular content even more rapidly than the Catholic schools. Unfortunately, "contentless" education seems to be as American as apple pie.

Be that as it may, there was still nothing at all wrong in

principle with a call for higher professional standards in Catholic education; rather the contrary. There is nothing better in its sphere than true professionalism in the sense of mastery of one's field and subject matter and acquired competence in applying them. It should always be part of the Christian vocation to be the best that one can be. The trouble was in the specific case of Catholic education, though, that the drive for greater professionalism coincided with the era of acute and growing discontent with any specifically Catholic education at all, as exemplified by Mary Perkins Ryan's *Are Parochial Schools the Answer?*. It also coincided with the growing flight from Creed, content, or message being promoted by the catechetical movement around the same time.

The result of it all was that when a greater professionalism did finally come to Catholic education, in particular Catholic religious education, it too often meant a systematic professional formation that included indoctrination in current anti-Church and anti-magisterium positions and attitudes—not to speak of growing disdain for the humble task of trying to pass on the inherited message at all. Sisters with a simple faith in Christ and his Church and a dedication to fostering the same kind of faith in their pupils would go off to a typical master's degree program or summer institute conducted by some of the fashionable theologians and catechetical experts and would return henceforth adamantly determined to offer every type of passive resistance to implementing practically anything whatever from the *General Catechetical Directory*, the U.S. bishops' 1973 *Basic Teachings for Catholic Religious Education*, the *National Catechetical Directory* when it finally came out in 1979, or Pope John Paul II's *Catechesi Tradendae*, issued in the same year.

This very same process of being "educated" out of one's faith apparently continues unabated today; one only has to leaf through *The National Catholic Reporter*'s annual issue of "Summer Listings" to note the kinds of courses typically being offered to teachers—and to note also the professors, too often open dissenters, teaching them. Nor is the process limited to religious sisters; far from it! It extends to nearly everyone in the field of religious education seeking enhanced professionalism and greater professional qualifications. There are some good schools, courses, and institutes, of course, but one usually has to know which ones they are; it is not apparent from the various announcements and advertisements. The system might as well have been designed expressly to perpetuate a religious education establishment hostile to the authentic Catholic tradition and the teachings of the Church's magisterium. And too often, no doubt, the bishops themselves continue to pay for having their professionals thus formed contrary to the mind of the Church.

Extraordinary as all this may seem, there is an even deeper level on which professionalism, understood as practitioners setting their own standards in their own fields, is simply incompatible with any direction from outside (meaning, in the Church) professionals declining to accept any outside direction from, say, bishops or pastors. Doctors or engineers, for example, normally set their own professional standards; nobody outside decrees what the treatment for arthritis must be or what the best method for constructing a suspension bridge is; professionals are autonomous in such matters. This is surely one of the important ways in which professionalism is understood in modern culture.

Now the modern idea of religious education as a profession has included a large measure of autonomy in precisely this same sense. Religious educators are tempted to see "the field" as belonging exclusively to them, not to the Church. It is a profession in which they—again not the Church—set the standards. Bishops and pastors do not know what they are doing and should stay out; they are not professionals. The professionals, and not the Church, must even be the ones to decide the content of religious education as well as the pedagogy, everything.

Today's religious educators sometimes see themselves as closer to other professional religious educators in other denominations than they do to their own co-religionists, to their own bishop or religious superior. Some of the modern anthologies on religious education include Catholics, Protestants, and Jews indiscriminately; such professionals, again, are working in "the field", and this sometimes takes precedence over whatever claims their faith community may have thought it had over them. For such professionals, Creeds, or articles of faith, can be of little importance compared to purely professional standards and training. There is, of course, a sense in which religious educators, as educators, can cooperate in certain ways across denominational lines, but this is not what is usually found today. What is found today is a demand for absolute autonomy for religious educators as professionals.

Anything less than autonomy would mean that religious education was not a true professional field, in other words, that it was not a profession; yet the first requirement is that it must be a profession; professionalism has become its essence. The same attitude, of course, is frequently encountered among modern theologians: scholars being by definition autonomous investigators, they *cannot* accept direction from the Church if they are going to remain scholars in the full sense of the word. It is bad enough when Catholic theologians adopt this attitude; it is worse when religious educators do, for then the very ones commissioned by the Church to hand on the faith are the ones who are undermining it by their declaration of independence from Church authority.

In order to confirm that this is indeed the attitude of many modern religious educators, determined above all to be recognized as professionals in the full sense of the word, it is worth quoting one of the more notable of modern catechetical theorists, Professor James Michael Lee. According to this theorist:

> A profession is characterized by autonomy. Unless the college or university enjoys autonomy it will tend to produce mindless drones instead of professionals. Any preparation program in religious education which is under the control of the bishop (such as the so-called "Catechetical Institutes" which have sprung up in some dioceses) or which is subject to the Curia (such as "Pontifical Institutes for Catechetics" that have been established in the United States and abroad) fails to meet the criteria of professional autonomy. Indeed, it probably is true that such operations do not aim to train professionals but rather individ-

> uals whose most outstanding competency is their ability to act in reflex agreement with ecclesiastical officials.[51]

It is hard to see how the point could have been stated more plainly. Anything less than acceptance of this point of view would apparently mean committing the teaching of the faith to "mindless drones" able and willing only to "act in reflex agreement with ecclesiastical officials". The implication is that true professionals would *not* so act in accord with ecclesiastical officials; there is not a hint of any responsibility or commitment to be made by the professionals in return for having the whole task of religious education delivered over into their hands; they are obligated by nothing, apparently, except by their own professionalism and what they autonomously decide.

In case there is any doubt about who would be in charge under such a regime of professional religious educators, a further quotation from the same catechetical theorist is quite revealing:

> Certification of a religion teacher should not be the prerogative of the local bishop or of the Vatican's Sacred Congregation for the Clergy as occurs in some dioceses of the United States and abroad. These officials lack the professional competence to make that kind or level of specialized judgment necessary for granting a license. Only a group formally representing the profession can properly issue a license to practice. Therefore the religious education profession should establish a licensing committee which will prepare, administer, and evaluate licensing examinations for persons seeking to become accredited religion teachers.[52]

According to this viewpoint, then, professional religious educators are the ones who should accredit and certify catechists. The religious education anthology from which the above quotations are taken included among its contributors an Episcopalian, a mainline Protestant, and an evangelical Christian, all of them religious educators; presumably they should have a say in certify-

[51] Lee, *Religious Education We Need,* p. 140.

[52] Ibid., p. 142.

ing catechists to teach the Catholic faith that is denied to the Catholic bishops, according to the above theory, since the former are professionals and the latter are not.

This understanding of professionalism is surely inherently subversive of the entire Catholic system, which, of course, makes bishops responsible both for the training of catechists and for granting them a mandate to teach; this is so fundamental a part of the Catholic system that one hardly knows which of so many Church documents to cite to establish the point (but it is made abundantly clear in chapter 3 of the *General Catechetical Directory,* for example, that the formation and commissioning of religion teachers is the "duty" of "bishops" and "ecclesiastical authorities", not of professionals, no matter what their training and competence). Yet it is the above understanding of professionalism that currently prevails among more Catholic religious educators than it is comfortable to think about; it may be contrary to the express teaching of the Church on the matter, but then religious educators have grown accustomed to the present climate of dissent in the Church where the express teaching of the Church does not necessarily decide anything or end any arguments.

Combined with the downgrading or abandonment of any definite Christian "doctrinal" message, and with the new and exaggerated emphasis on human psychology and experience, this kind of understanding of the new professionalism is one of the principal things that has helped make a shambles of religious education in the Catholic Church in the United States over the past quarter of a century.

6.

Is Catholic religious education in the United States in shambles at the present time? The dictionary defines "shambles" as a place where butchers kill animals, a slaughterhouse. Thus, by extension, a shambles is something marked by great disorder or destruction. In spite of the many bright spots that it is always *de rigueur* to mention, in spite of the many dedicated catechists, teachers, directors of religious education, pastors, and bishops who have remained in place and who go on doing their proper job of proclaiming and teaching the true faith of Christ exactly as the Church wishes and requires, it nevertheless has to be admitted that, yes, there has been considerable "disorder" and even "destruction" in religious education in the United States over the past twenty-five years or so—some of it beginning even before the Council. Some of this "disorder" and "destruction" in catechesis has been described and documented in the course of the present study, and there is more to come.

It was once shrewdly prophesied: "The time will come when people will not tolerate sound doctrine, but, following their own desires, will surround themselves with teachers who tickle their ears. They will stop listening to the truth and will wander off to fables" (2 Tim 4:3–4). This quotation from the New Testament is not only a good description of what has occurred in large sectors of Catholic religious education in the United States in the postconciliar era, but it is close to being a meticulously precise description! From the generalized discontent with so much that was Catholic that characterized so many Catholics as Vatican II got underway, especially among the educated and actual or would-be sophisticated and professionals among them, the slide into the new variant religion featuring emphasis upon social reform and betterment and upon personal psychology, guided by a wholly modern and secular professionalism, was very rapid. Catechesis was quickly stripped of its traditional content based on the transmitted faith of the Church and began to reflect these other, predominantly human and worldly emphases.

What was even more strange than the fact that all this occurred, though, was how little anyone, including especially anyone in authority in the Church, with rare exception, ever seemed to notice or, at any rate, to admit, that it was occurring or had occurred—or, especially, how necessarily destructive what was occurring was of authentic faith. Prominent religious educators could declare their complete independence of the authority of the Church, indeed of the doctrine of the faith itself, and people would go right on considering them prominent "Catholic religious educators", apparently in good standing and with untarnished reputations. Textbooks could be completely subversive of the Catholic faith and yet go right on being used and praised as if they were the old Baltimore Catechism itself. Meanwhile it was not only not respectable, it was more than faintly disreputable even to raise questions about what was going on; anyone temerarious enough to attempt it was usually immediately branded "right wing", "extremist", and, of course, "mean-spirited".

This was not the whole picture, of course. As will be chronicled at some length in the next chapter, there was a long succession of serious official efforts on the part of the authorities of the Church to correct the deficiencies that were indeed perceived to be present in the new catechesis; these official efforts mainly consisted in the preparation and issuance of successive official documents, some of them outstanding documents, right on the mark, specifying what religious education ought to consist of in the Church. The issuance of each of these new documents in turn was supposed to be corrective of the situation preceived to be in need of correction; yet the fact that another such document was always in preparation within another year or two always proved that the situation had not in fact been corrected. Meanwhile there was another tendency present in the attitude of the authorities of the Church, and that was to reaffirm blandly from time to time that nothing really essential was amiss with religious education. Yes, mistakes had been made; some unfortunate experimentation had gone on; perhaps the attitude of religious educators was not always what it should be—but all these things would no doubt be corrected following the issuance of the next Church document on the subject.

There is space here to instance only one religious educator and one religion textbook to illustrate the main point being made here, namely, that Church authorities never really followed up in practice to insure that religion teachers were actually following the prescriptions found in their documents and that religion textbooks reflected in their content these same prescriptions.

1. *A Religious Educator.*

For many years Brother Gabriel Moran was one of the biggest "names" in catechesis in the United States. Long a Christian Brother and head of a province of the Christian Brothers, he later became a professor of religious education at New York University. The 1983 Sourcebook for Modern Catechetics described his contributions to and position in the catechetical movement as follows:

> Few persons in the United States have made a contribution to the catechetical scene as complex and difficult to assess as Gabriel Moran, currently professor of religious education at New York University. In 1966, the publication of his Catholic University doctoral dissertation in two volumes, *Theology of Revelation* and *Catechesis of Revelation,* popularized the catechetical renewal at the same time it severely criticized some of its errors. By means of these two books, his thought influenced catechesis worldwide.[53]

No doubt in view of his perceived importance in the catechetical movement, Gabriel Moran, in the 1980s, was asked to revise, update, and comment upon for inclusion in the rather comprehensive *Sourcebook for Modern Catechetics* itself, a 1970 *Commonweal* article of his that had been published under the title, "Catechetics, R.I.P.", an article that had created something of a sensation when it was first published. The clear implication of this request to Gabriel Moran more than a dozen years later to rework this article for publication in book form was that the article in some way represented a valid contribution to Catholic catechesis; this was the case, apparently, even though the article in question had advanced such theses as that "anyone who sets out to educate in the field of religion has to put Scripture, liturgy, and Christian theology in a broader context that does not afford Christianity a normative role". The article also accused what the author called "right wingers" of wasting "their energies searching out heresy at a time when that problem has been

[53] Warren, ed., *Sourcebook,* p. 290.

swallowed up by the much larger question of the existence of any Christianity at all".[54]

If words mean anything, these words surely mean that "Christianity", in the view of the author, was no longer to be considered "normative", that is, prescriptive or governing in catechesis; "Christianity", in other words, was no longer to be taught in catechesis *as true.* Over a century ago in his famous "Biglietto Speech", delivered on the occasion of receiving his red hat, Cardinal John Henry Newman had predicted that what he called "religious liberalism" would eventually bring about a situation where Christianity would no longer be taught as true, but not even Cardinal Newman probably ever imagined that representatives of official Catholic catechesis would ever *accept* that kind of teaching; he little reckoned either on a "Catholic religious educator" advancing such a thesis or the acceptance of such a thesis for inclusion in a Catholic *Sourcebook for Modern Catechetics.* Yet when all this occurred with the publication of that book there is no record that any eyebrows were even raised.

Indeed, once again, if words mean anything, there even seems to have been serious question in Gabriel Moran's mind whether or not there actually existed anything that properly could be called Christianity at all. At any rate, whatever Christianity may have been thought to be, it was not what established the subject matter of "religious education", the author's professional "field", in which he was an acknowledged expert.

Can this be right? An author repudiates Christianity itself, yet not only goes on considering himself a Catholic religious educator but continues to be considered one by others as well, to the point that he is included as a contributor in a comprehensive anthology on the subject published over a decade after his repudiation of Christianity.

In order to verify that this is not an inexact or unfair characterization of the position of this particular "acknowledged expert" in Catholic religious education, it is only necessary to turn to another

[54] Ibid., pp. 295–96.

book published by Gabriel Moran in 1972, a book called *The Present Revelation.* This book begins with the flat statement, which the author himself warns should not be "dismissed as a piece of exaggeration and sensationalism", that "there is a middle generation of American Roman Catholics who no longer believe anything". By page 3 of the book it appears that Catholicism has quite simply broken up: "The break-up of Roman Catholicism has been more rapid than anyone could have expected." By page 5 the author has declared that truth itself is impossible to attain: "Every objectified expression of truth is also laden with an element of doubt" (except, no doubt, the "truth" asserted by the author that the Catholic Church had long since become "a non-credible institution") and that, since the nineteenth century, all knowledge had become "relativized", including especially religious knowledge of the type the official documents of the Catholic Church continue to specify must be the basis and form the content of all the Church's catechesis.

For this author, though, there was already nothing left that could be firmly believed, and since that was the case, it apparently followed for him that his entire generation of Catholics had to "suspend" belief. However, many of them, including presumably the author himself, still continued to "care for the tradition". This, then, is how it was possible to consider oneself a Catholic religious educator even after repudiating Christianity itself: one continued to care for the tradition. However else such a position might be characterized, it is certainly Catholicism entirely on one's own terms, bearing no relationship to the requirements the Church lays down for authentic Catholicism. The author's reasoning, though, was as follows:

> Suppose that one neither accepts nor rejects Christianity? Suppose one has an affinity for a Christian life but finds the concept of a "Christian revelation" to be unintelligible? Suppose that one finds Christianity to be an inescapable element of one's life and that one approaches it with care and intelligence but that one cannot possibly believe that it (or anything else) is the norm of one's life. By the standards of ecclesiastical definition

one is not a Christian and according to Christian theology one is not a theologian. However, these very definitions could use challenging from some other set of premises.[55]

Thus, even admitting that "by the standards of ecclesiastical definition one is no longer a Christian", one need not, for all of that, withdraw from the field of religious education, since these same standards of ecclesiastical definition could "use challenging" anyway. It is quite clear that in the postconciliar era they *have* been challenged as a matter of fact, and by a "generation of Catholics who no longer believe anything [but] still remain Catholic", according to this author.[56]

It is interesting with what confidence this author asserts that an entire generation of Catholics no longer believes in the Church; the assertion was delivered as if the author, and not the magisterium of the Church, was the one who enjoyed the special assistance of the Holy Spirit; and it is especially interesting considering that the same author believes that nothing at all can be known with certainty anyway, even including, presumably, the assertion that a whole generation of Catholics no longer believe.

It is hard enough to credit that anyone holding such views should even continue to be considered a Catholic, let alone a religious educator in good standing. Yet the really huge irony here is that, over the past couple of decades, Catholic religious educators have often been more ready to listen to and be guided by a Gabriel Moran than by the voice of the Church specifying what was to be taught in religious education. As these pages were being written, nearly thirty years after his famous *Commonweal* article "Catechetics, R.I.P." commemorating the apparent demise of any Catholic religious education at all, Gabriel Moran apparently continues to be one of the professors featured at the kind of "Summer Institute" to which bishops and religious superiors con-

[55] Moran, *Present Revelation,* pp. 3, 5, 12, 14–15.
[56] Ibid., p. 12.

tinue to send their catechists and religion teachers for more training and indoctrination "in the field".[57]

2. *A Religion Textbook*

It is not possible for the present study to go into detail regarding the deficiencies of the new religion textbooks in use over the past quarter of a century. That vexed subject could easily require a whole book and more in its own right. Most of the controversies over religious education since Vatican II, in fact, have focused on the textbooks; reams of ad hoc analyses and critiques have been prepared and turned in to bishops, pastors, and religious education offices about them. The typical and recurring complaint about the books is that they do not "teach the faith", that they contain omissions, distortions, and even errors of Catholic doctrine. Another word frequently used to describe typical new religion textbooks has been "mush".

Religious educators have typically defended quite vigorously both the new kinds of religion textbooks in use and the methods used to teach them. They have typically dismissed the complaints against them as merely "differences" from the way religion used to be taught out of the Baltimore Catechism. They have reacted in this fashion, no doubt, because the new religion textbooks are commonly integral products of the catechetical movement in which most of the educators too have been trained, hence defense of the religion textbooks under attack amounts to defense of the new catechesis itself. Even when they have been forced to admit the existence of real concern over the books in use, as when the U.S. bishops came out with their *Basic Teachings on Catholic Religious Education,* the religious educators have usually just staged a tactical retreat, granting the existence of "concern" and paying lip service to the necessity of "sound doctrine". Year after year,

[57] See the advertisement for Boston College's 1991 Summer Institute in *Commonweal,* September 14, 1990, where Gabriel Moran was listed as one of the professors on the subject of "Current Issues in Religious Education".

however, with rare exceptions, little has been improved in the new religion textbooks since they first started being published around the time of the Council, for the fact is that modern religion teachers firmly believe in what they have been doing, regardless of what Rome, the American bishops, or Catholic parents may think, and the books that get published, get on the "approved lists" of religious education offices, and thus get into the classrooms tend to be the ones inspired by the catechetical movement and approved of by the professionals. Only very recently, in fact, have the U.S. bishops been concerned with the publication of religion textbooks at all.[58]

The end result of this state of affairs has been that many diocesan "approved lists" of religion textbooks and religious education materials contain nothing but the typical creedless and contentless type of books characteristic of the new catechesis, only minimally modified to take into account the continuing complaints of parents, pastors, many, many teachers, and even bishops over the past couple of decades since all of the controversies over religion textbooks first began. Conversely, "orthodox" religion textbook series, such as those published by the Daughters of Saint Paul or Ignatius Press, are too often, unaccountably, deliberately left off these "approved lists". The votaries of the new catechesis who usually staff these religious education offices are able to see to that. And when the criticisms persist, as they do, the experts parry with slogans such as "books don't teach religion; teachers do"! (Yes, but what if the teacher has been trained by, say, Gabriel Moran?)

Meanwhile the bishops, uneasy with the incessant controversy over religious education, from time to time have issued their guidelines such as the *Basic Teachings for Catholic Religious Education* and the *National Catechetical Directory* that will be described in the next chapter. The fact that, by 1985, the Synod of Bishops found it necessary to call for a Catechism for the Universal Church meant that the situation continued to remain fundamentally

[58] See the U.S. bishops' "Guidelines on Doctrine for Catechetical Materials", *Origins*, CNS Documentary Service, December 13, 1990.

uncorrected; and this remains the case today, while the final and definitive version of this Catechism is being completed. The fact is that the statements and guidance issued by the bishops on this subject, however sound they have been (and they have been), never really got to the root of the problem. The root of the problem resides in the fact that the Church's formal religious education has been placed in, and has remained in, the hands of typical products of a world catechetical movement that long ago lost interest in teaching the Catholic faith as the Church wishes it to be taught; the catechetical movement went on to other things long ago, as has been indicated in the course of this study.

Of course the typical religious educators have never stated in so many words: "We are not really interested any longer in teaching the faith as handed down in the Church, and, even if we were, we are now wedded to methods and textbooks that would make it impossible to teach it in any case." No such admirable frankness or candor has characterized the typical modern religious educators, and hence what they are really doing can only be determined by observation and by studying the typical textbooks and other products of their movement. Since the bishops, like the Catholic people, have generally neglected to do that, the typical encounter with someone who has been initiated into the catechetical movement's principles and assumptions has generally been a baffling one; it is normally very hard to understand where these people are coming from.

Nevertheless some of the typical products are there for anyone who will take the trouble to look at them. Particularly notable have been the new religion textbooks. As already indicated, it is possible here to look at only one example of a modern textbook that is defective from the standpoint of properly transmitting the faith of the Church. The text in question is *Christ among Us,* by Anthony Wilhelm.[59] This book is of particular interest. After it had been in common use for over a decade as a very popular basic

[59] Anthony J. Wilhelm, *Christ among Us: A Modern Presentation of the Catholic Faith,* 2d rev. ed. (New York and Paramus, N.J.: Paulist Press, 1975).

text on the Catholic faith for adult inquirers, the Congregation for the Doctrine of the Faith (CDF), in one of the few cases of its kind where the CDF proceeded against a single book, requested that the book's *Imprimatur,* or permission to be printed with ecclesiastical approval, be removed. The Archdiocese of Newark promptly complied, and the book's *Imprimatur* was accordingly removed.

However, this did not have the effect of removing the book from circulation or use as a religion text. According to a story in the *New York Times,*[60] a secular publisher, Harper and Row, immediately decided to reissue the book without any *Imprimatur.* It had sold over a million copies since 1968, it was very readable, and it was considered the best introduction to the Catholic faith on the market—despite the fact that the Church's highest doctrinal authority had declared it to be unsuitable for teaching the authentic Catholic faith. It apparently continued to sell quite briskly after it was republished without ecclesiastical approval. An ad appearing in *Commonweal* magazine in December 1990 described yet another new edition of the same book in the following terms: "*Christ among Us* is today's most widely read introduction to Catholicism. Newly revised and updated, with an appendix for use with the Rite of Christian Initiation for Adults (RCIA), this up-to-the-minute survey of modern Catholicism addresses the questions of doctrine, traditions, and contemporary practice that are of concern to all adult inquirers—including those reexamining their Catholic faith." Blurbs accompanying this ad included the *New York Times'* characterization of the book as "the nation's most widely used introduction to Catholicism" and the U.S. bishops' own Catholic News Service endorsement of the book as "a fine piece of scholarship".[61]

What kind of a book is it that, even though it has been condemned by the Catholic Church's highest doctrinal authority,

[60] *New York Times,* November 29, 1984.

[61] "New from Harper San Francisco", ad in *Commonweal,* December 7, 1990. The same advertisement includes a strong plug for *The Universal Catechism Reader,* edited by Thomas J. Reese, S.J.

continues to be "the nation's most widely used introduction to Catholicism"? To look, even sketchily, at the contents of this book is to begin to understand something about what has too often been wrong with Catholic religion textbooks generally in the postconciliar era.

Christ among Us is a well-written and well-organized book that attempts to treat the subject of Christ and salvation history in depth.[62] It not only treats these subjects, it also offers within the book itself many teaching aids that make the book an attractive textbook: emphases within the text of important points, questions at the end of each chapter, applications in the liturgy and in the personal life of the student, and suggestions for further readings, related filmstrips, and movies. All these features no doubt help account for the book's popularity. The author has written the book also in a popular and easy to understand style, yet it has a certain dignity to it. It is not slangy and "with it" to an offensive degree the way some other modern religion textbooks attempt to be.

The author states that he is giving a contemporary presentation of Catholicism based on Scripture and the Second Vatican Council (p. 3). He tries to show the reader "how our worship expresses our belief" (p. 3), and he has similarly tried to incorporate modern ecumenical viewpoints. He also states that the work is necessarily "transitional and tentative: we ask those who use this book to bear in mind that this an interim effort. It might well be an overly audacious, even foolhardy attempt to speak about God and his revelation at a time when Christianity is undergoing a universal questioning and theology a massive reconstruction. . . . Today nothing is more apparent than that we know very little indeed" (p. 3).

This attitude of tentativeness is evident in the way the author consistently treats his subject matter: no *kerygma,* or proclamation, here. Also, the modern Church exhibits no such hesitation in proclaiming her full faith as Wilhelm manifests throughout; the fact is that he is unwilling to allow the Church or the Scriptures to teach definitely and "with authority".

[62] Wilhelm, *Christ among Us.*

To begin with the Church: in approaching this topic, the author often presents the authentic teaching of the Church, but then he goes on to surround it with so many qualifications that it no longer seems so authentic or plausible after all; it too becomes tentative. Again, "we know very little indeed." But faith in the good news is not a matter of "knowing" something in the sense of having successfully researched it; anyone comparing this book to any of the books in the New Testament will immediately notice the difference in tone and atmosphere.

Although the author mentions infallibility and the teaching authority of the Church in various places throughout the book, he deals with them specifically in chapter 10 under the title "Those Who Serve as Our Guides". This chapter is quite interesting to read, and it makes many accurate statements about the teaching Church, but these statements, once again, are rarely left standing alone. For example on page 138, Wilhelm says: "Peter went eventually to Rome where his position as leader of the early Christian Church was passed on to his successors, the bishops of Rome. Peter's leadership is evident in the early Church, yet not as one endowed with supreme jurisdiction; all the apostles had been commissioned by Christ and evidently felt little need to refer to Peter." Thus, the author states that Peter was the recognized leader in the early Church, but then he immediately qualifies it; it turns out that Peter was a leader with very little authority after all; the apostles felt little need to refer to him, just as, presumably, modern bishops should feel little need to refer to Peter's successor.

Another example of Wilhelm's manner of proceeding can be found on page 141: "The pre-eminent authority of the Roman Church was recognized from the early centuries by most of the Christian world. . . . It was the only one recognized as universal leader, at least to some extent, by the Christian world in general." Thus, here again, it is established that the Roman Church was a universal leader, but then the author says Rome's position in this regard was not so preeminent after all.

When he comes to the issue of infallibility, Wilhelm once again states it correctly: "To be sure men would get his message and to avoid confusion, Christ gave his Church infallibility. Infallibility means Christ's guidance of the Church through the Holy Spirit so that it cannot make a mistake in teaching his message" (p. 147). However, by the time page 150 is reached infallibility turns out to be of very little practical help in safeguarding Christ's message after all: "By its infallibility, the Church does not claim to possess the whole truth of God and his relationship to man, but only what we humans are able to see of his revelation *at this particular point in history*" (emphasis added). Presumably with on-going revelation, it will all eventually come out. Meanwhile, so much for Christ's guidance of the Church through the Holy Spirit! "Actually", it turns out, "the Church's infallible teachings, which give us a measure of certainty in our service of God, say very little" (p. 150).

When he deals with Scripture, Wilhelm is equally tentative. On the one hand, he states on page 21: "While the Bible's purpose is religious, its basic story is an accurate history." On the other hand, he has no qualms at all about stating that the authors of the New Testament had no interest in facts: "They are not greatly concerned about when or where a thing happened, the details of what happened, the exact words Christ used, etc." (p. 66). This, of course, is the viewpoint of those scholars who think the Gospels were all written late and composed using "legends" accumulated in the early Church.

When dealing with the resurrection of Christ, however, an event that receives more direct, unequivocal, and unadorned support than any other happening in the Bible—for example, 1 Corinthians 12:24; all the four Gospels are built around the fact of the resurrection and of the original *kerygma* of that event; Acts is similarly constructed around it—Wilhelm arrives again at a wholly tentative conclusion that again represents a favorite notion of a certain type of modern Scripture scholar even while it is quite plainly at variance with the entire Catholic tradition: "To believe in Christ's divinity one must have an open mind and a willingness to live his teachings—and the power of faith. Sceptics, those whose minds are closed to his teachings or to moral improvement, like Herod, Pontius Pilate, and the Pharisees, *probably would have seen nothing* had they been with the Apostles when Christ appeared after his resurrection" (p. 89; emphasis added). This view is entirely fanciful, of course, whatever Scripture scholars may claim; such a view is based not on any hard evidence from the Gospels themselves, which unequivocally affirm the objective reality of the resurrection, but rather is based upon the a priori modern belief that the resurrection could not have occurred and that the Gospels' affirmation of it was therefore necessarily based on some subjective experiences of the risen Jesus on the part of the apostles. All of the available evidence concerning the resurrection—necessarily from the New Testament—points to the fact that it really did occur; and if it is true evidence, as the Church holds, then anybody who was with the apostles would have seen something.

With regard to the author's treatment of Scripture generally, it is entirely legitimate to be concerned with the intent of the authors of the various books of the Bible and with the literary forms that were used, and so on; the Church encourages this type of study. But Anthony Wilhelm throughout tends to ignore the real intent of the evangelists (for example, Lk 1:1–4), as well as the clear teaching of the Church to the effect that "Holy Mother Church has firmly and with absolute constancy held, and continues to hold, that the four Gospels . . . whose historical character the Church unhesitatingly asserts, faithfully hand on what Jesus Christ, while living among men, really did and taught for their eternal salvation until the day he was taken up into heaven" (Vatican II, *Dei Verbum,* no. 19).

Similarly, with regard to Christ himself, the same pattern continues. Wilhelm says many good things about Christ and brings out certain orthodox points about him, but the overall context in which Christ is situated lacks some essential things. As already indicated, the certainty of magisterial and scriptural teaching is often undermined. In addition, Wilhelm has adopted an evolutionary view of reality that makes the role of a Redeemer seem almost redundant. To give one example from the book, on page 22, the author states: "The Bible's account of creation can fit in perfectly with science's teaching on the evolution of the universe. . . . God brings the world to realization, not by continual interventions—stepping in to 'make' this or that—but in such a way that the higher emerges from the lower, by evolution. He is continually creating as he activates the whole gigantic, unfolding process." Again, on page 24, the book states: "Each person's soul or spiritual power comes specially from God, but not by God's intervening and putting something in as from the outside. Our soul does not exist before we do as a person. Each person's soul is a special 'aspect' of God's continuing creation of the universe—an individual spiritual power that comes about by the evolutionary process which God began, working out itself in each of us." Or again, on page 34: "God's grace-presence gives us the power to transform everything we do into eternal happiness for ourselves and others. . . . God's plan was that man would develop so that he could have his grace-presence, grow in it, and be with him forever in heaven. He would send his son, Jesus Christ, to earth when men were ready, to fill us with a superabundance of his grace-presence." The author uses Christian-sounding terms here—"grace", "God's son", and so on—but transforms their meaning strangely in accordance with a vision of his own; it is certainly *not* Catholicism.

"At the end there will be a new universe—a new heaven and a new earth", the author asserts. "The universe is now 'in labor' towards this better state. . . . There will be a vast cosmic renewal and glorification, and God will be revealed in all things, present among us in undreamed of ways. . . . *It is up to us to bring about this new universe*" (p. 423–24; emphasis added).

The strong evolutionary thread that runs through this whole book makes the moral and physical improvement of man seem either inevitable—just part of an on-going process—or else dependent upon man to help himself, with perhaps just a little help and encouragement from Jesus. The whole point of salvation history and the need for a Redeemer is vitiated by this kind of treatment. While developing these dominant evolutionary ideas, Wilhelm ends up downgrading or even contradicting some essential Christian doctrines, including the doctrine of original sin, which he defines, typically, as "the accumulated sin of mankind" (p. 37), and including also the original state of holiness in which Adam and Eve lived, indeed, even the very existence of these first parents: "Is God saying that they were created in a state of sublime happiness and grace from which they fell? This has been the traditional view, but the biblical imagery probably refers to the ideal to be sought after, rather than describing something that actually once existed" (p. 35). How easy it is, it always turns out, to set aside what is called "the traditional view".

However, the existence—and fall—of a first human couple is in no way merely a "traditional view"; it is the teaching of the Church, to be found most recently in Pope Paul VI's 1968 Profession of Faith, or Credo of the People of God:

> We believe that in Adam all have sinned, which means the original offense committed by him caused human nature, common to all men, to fall to a state in which it bears the consequences of that offense, and which is not the state in which it was at first in our first parents, established as they were in holiness and justice, and in which man knew neither evil nor death. It is human nature so fallen, stripped of the grace that clothed it, injured in its own natural powers and subject to the dominion of death, that is transmitted to all men, and it is in this sense that every man is born in sin. We, therefore, hold, with the Council of Trent, that original sin is transmitted with human nature, "not by imitation but by propagation" and it is "proper to everyone".

If, as Anthony Wilhelm seems to assume, human beings live in a world in which the higher is automatically emerging from the lower, in which man is not in a fallen state as a result of original sin, but is rather currently at the highest point of his development, and in which problems only arise because men do not strive hard enough to bring about the creation of a new, perfected earth, then the functional role of the Redeemer has got to be somewhat different from the one assigned to Christ in the Old and New

Testaments, in the formal dogmas of the Catholic Church, and in the beliefs of Christians over the last two millenia.

In chapter 8, "Christ Saves Us by His Death and Resurrection", Wilhelm, following his usual pattern, initially describes the redemptive function of Christ reasonably well: "God sent his own Son, Jesus Christ, to overcome the power of sin and fill us with his grace-presence" (p. 102); "By dying for us Christ made up for our sins" (p. 103); "We call Jesus Christ the King of the universe, of angels and of men, because all things belong to him as God, and because as man he redeemed us" (p. 113). In the same chapter, however, he makes statements that do not fit into this redemptive framework at all but rather into an evolutionary framework in which a Redeemer is truly incidental—a framework in which the perfection of this world is inevitably being achieved, and mainly by human effort. "It is becoming more and more apparent", the author writes, "that God cannot be expected to intervene in our affairs with displays of power—that his followers are decreasing in worldly and institutional importance—but by this apparent absence from the world he is prodding us to use our human resources to work with him to bring it to perfection. . . . 'God is teaching us that we must live as men who can get along very well without him. . . .' " (p. 110). It is hard to understand how anyone could ascribe the foregoing sentence to the same religion whose Founder taught that "apart from me you can do nothing" (Jn 15:5).

Or again: "He is personally giving us all the graces by which we attain heaven and by which we bring others and the universe itself to perfection" (p. 114). The emphasis here has clearly been changed from salvation from sin to the perfection of the present world—where, in fact, "we have no lasting city" (Heb 13:14).

This religion textbook by Anthony Wilhelm is typical of many modern religion textbooks in that it uses Christian terminology—"grace", "heaven", and so on—but fits them into a totally different framework than the framework of historic Christianity or Catholicism.

More could be said about this book, much more, in fact; but what has been said should suffice. It seems pretty clear that anyone using this book would probably end up very confused about just who Jesus Christ is. He might grasp that Jesus was an unusual person of great abilities and influence, but it is hard to say what other firm conclusions about Jesus he might be able to arrive at on the basis of the kind of confused and sometimes contradictory information provided in this religion text, "today's most widely read introduction to Catholicism". Any book with the title *Christ among Us* needed to do better than that.

7.

The disarray that religious education has too often become in the postconciliar era still remains in need of efficacious remedies. Very little has effectively been done to move the catechetical movement back to a God-centered and Christ-centered perspective from the humanistic and this-worldly perspective that that movement adopted from the 1960s on; religious educators and religion texts still reflect in much too great a degree this same emphasis, along with reliance on psychological and experiential methods quite unsuited to handing on the tenets of a faith revealed "once and for all". Meanwhile adherence to a kind of professionalism that resists guidance and direction from the authority of the Church is only strengthened when prestigious theologians, functioning as a para-magisterium, offer religious educators another view of the faith and their task in transmitting it—a view that, in their current state of mind, seems more in keeping with the way they think things ought to be.

Yet the disarray that religious education has too often become can be assessed in another way, other than by looking at these existing trends, as has been done in the course of the present chapter; the confusion in question can best be assessed by applying the most fundamental of all tests: results. Do those who have been taught or catechized, namely, contemporary students, know and practice their faith? What are the indications here?

Of course people today do have a strong subjective impression that "the kids don't know their faith". There are many signs of that. Beyond such impressions however, the answer to these questions has been pretty definitively established and verified for well over a decade. The answer—in case anybody had any doubt about it—is: No! Many of those who have been catechized and taught in formal Catholic religion programs do *not* know and practice their faith adequately by almost any measurable standard. This should hardly surprise anyone who has read this far in the present study.

With controversies over religion teaching and religion textbooks raging all around, it was inevitable, in this age of polls, surveys, and studies, that efforts would be made to determine with some degree of objectivity the effectiveness of the new catechesis. This chapter will conclude by summarizing the results of one of the major efforts made along these lines.

In the spring of 1976, a special task force of the National Catholic Education Association was convened to prepare a Religious Education Outcomes Inventory (REOI) consisting of a ninety-item religious knowledge inventory and a forty-item religious/moral catalogue. The religious knowledge inventory was designed to yield individual and class profiles in five areas: (1) God, Father, Son, and Spirit; (2) Church, Community of Believers; (3) Sacraments, Initiation, Community, and Reconciliation; (4) Christian Life, Witness and Service; and (5) Scripture, Living Word of God. The attitude measure was to report, item by item, group responses on attitudes relating to the same five areas.

Drawing upon the *General Catechetical Directory,* a current draft of what would become the *National Catechetical Directory,* the U.S. bishops' 1973 instruction *Basic Teachings for Catholic Religious Education,* the U.S. bishops' 1972 pastoral letter *To Teach as Jesus Did,* the *NCEA Curriculum Guide for Continuous Progress in Religious Education Programs,* and major religion textbooks in current use, the special NCEA task force selected the contents and items for the REOI. This instrument was designed for use by school and CCD programs on the junior high, but ideally on the eighth grade, levels. Generally accepted by school administrators and personnel, the utilization of the inventory was initially, and continued to be, challenged by a number of professionals responsible for nonschool religious education programs, locally and nationally. By 1980, the REOI had already been administered to over 100,000 students from nearly one hundred dioceses and some two thousand institutions across the country.

What were some of the results? Writing in the June 1978 *NCEA Religious Education Forum Newsletter,* Father Alfred McBride, O.Praem., who was the NCEA Religious Education Forum director at the time, presented a report on the REOI results of 1978. What follows are a number of key areas that Father McBride said were in need of a good deal more attention and work. Indeed, his results were quite sobering in their implications and are therefore worth quoting at some length:

> For the second year in a row, students appear to falter when faced with religious code words (eternal life, ecumenism, grace).... Here I wish to draw your attention to the matter of what some call a religious 'illiteracy' among our young Catholics. One cannot conclude from the REOI that a working vocabulary for young Catholics is not being taught. But one could infer that many of them are not aware of the code words. Frankly, they are not learning the words, let alone the content and meaning of the terms.... Such competence ought to be the sign of a trained, informed, and literate Catholic.... Obviously, I see no point in just mastering a list of items with little or no reference to their meaning and significance for Christian attitudes and practice. My point is that the inability to know the concepts, carefully honed into terms understood by the Catholic Community, leads to a foolish and unnecessary breakdown in communication. Not to do so is to require of religion a childish simplicity which would not be tolerated by any other form of study or behavior. History, Science, English, Sociology all have their own code words as a shorthand for talking about the topic. To ignore this in religion is to make Christianity some kind of unearthly, pre-literate experience above and beyond the mere learning of terms that lesser disciplines, in their presumably unenlightened way, must cope with. Some counter at this point that there is no right definition of terms, that the new pluralism refuses to box concepts in that way. Everything is a

kind of open-endedness that will not tolerate such confinement. The only thing I can say is nonsense and rubbish!

Liturgy—definitely the weakest aspect of performance at the moment. And all the more surprising since talk about liturgy seems to be at an all-time high. Despite this, the students are fuzzy and imprecise about the meaning and purpose of many of the sacraments.... Much laughter was generated in the past decade about identifying sacraments in Baltimore Catechism terms. But when the laughter has quieted down, it may be sobering to note that they do not know to identify them in post-Vatican-II terms, ones which *do* have a consensus. The institutional language has been replaced with appealing talk about encounters with Christ. Appealing it may be, but the students have not yet assimilated this at the level of concept. (We can make no judgment about other ways of assimilation other than to note that language is the window of the mind and when one sees only a mist inside, it causes one to ponder....) .... They seem to get the fellowship/community aspects of Church life, but it seems a folly to leave them with the impression that there is no system and order in the Church. The Church is both community and institution. The richer view should produce more balanced Catholics. REOI indicates that such a balance must yet be sought. Most of them appear never to have heard of Eastern Uniate Catholics and they would give the Holy Father and bishops pause, were their grasp of teaching authority no better than their current performance.

Regarding the Scriptures, REOI shows that students do not know the major differences between the two Testaments. They have not mastered the small skill of reading a Bible citation nor how to interpret one of the Bible's easiest passages, Mt 25, on the last judgment. As for doctrine, students still think the Immaculate Conception is the Virgin Birth. Grace remains a mystery for them even as an identifiable term. Sad to say they have neither a pre- nor a post-Vatican-II appreciation of miracles and find the resurrection of the dead as puzzling as an obscure term found in the *New York Times* Sunday crossword puzzle. They have yet to find a way of decoding eternal life and the significance of faith as a gift. I would never claim that such lofty doctrines ought to be grasped in depth by young students.

It is not a question of depth perception so much as any perception at all. The great Christian doctrines will always keep us in awe and silence before the mystery. But we need to know what to be in awe about.

On marriage many of them moved away from having children to showing love as the primary purpose. Presumably marriage is not yet a top priority for such young ones; still they seem to have caught a disjointed vision of its purpose.... On the positive side, they do seem to be aware of the meaning of Original Sin, know the list of the Ten Commandments, appreciated marriage as a union of the couple with each other and Christ, and can give a central description of the process of salvation. In fact, on over half the items they did quite well.[63]

Not an entirely negative picture, then, but not much of an endorsement of the new catechesis, either. This account of the outcomes of one of the first major studies of the new religious education has been quoted at some length, because of how well its story is told as well as because of the story itself. Its author, Father Alfred McBride, was himself prominent on the catechetical scene during the period covered, and it is a tribute to his honesty and integrity that he was able and willing to draw the conclusions he drew from the data before him. Too many, contrary to the predominance of evidence, continue to maintain that there is nothing fundamentally wrong with the direction taken by Catholic religious education since the Council.

However that may be, the next chapter will cover the succession of official efforts carried out by Church authorities to try to remedy the continuing perceived deficiencies in carrying out the Church's mission of handing on her own faith. Given the existence of these deficiencies—which, by now, have been abundantly documented—there is little wonder that a Catechism for the Universal Church should have finally come to be thought necessary.

[63] Father Alfred McBride, O.Praem., "Less than 60%... Or Everything You Didn't Want to Know about Their Answers", in *NCEA Religious Education Forum Newsletter,* June 1978.

Chapter III

Official Efforts by the Hierarchy to Remedy Cathechetical Deficiencies

I.

The Second Vatican Council officially closed on the Feast of the Immaculate Conception, December 8, 1965. As Pope John Paul II was later to remark in his 1979 apostolic exhortation *Catechesi Tradendae,* Pope Paul VI, the pope who, under Providence, brought this Ecumenical Council begun by his predecessor, Pope John XXIII, to a successful conclusion, saw Vatican II as itself "the great catechism of modern times".[1]

It was a catechism, though, that time would shortly prove many sons and daughters of the Church were failing to study or heed very carefully. The many changes in the Church's practices and discipline (not her teachings) that the Council legitimately decreed heralded another era of further changes improvised by individuals on their own in accordance with something they often called "the spirit of Vatican II", but really in accordance with ideas promoted by a new theology that progressively had been cutting its ties with the tradition and magisterium of the Catholic Church. Often the Catholic faithful could not distinguish which of the many changes were authentic—that is, had been decreed by the legitimate authority of the Church—and which were improvisations and abuses—that is, launched by individuals on their own whim and initiative, usually in response to the latest theological fad. In the course of the twenty-five years following the end of the Council, much of the confusion generated after Vatican II did

[1] Pope John Paul II, Apostolic Exhortation *Catechesi Tradendae* on Catechesis in Our Time, October 16, 1979, no. 2.

manage to get itself sorted out, sometimes quite favorably. Unhappily, this proved to be generally somewhat less true in catechesis, or the teaching of the faith, than it did in some other areas of the Church's life. Twenty-five years after the end of the Council, the Church was still sorely in need of a Catechism for the Universal Church to set an unchallengeable standard.

The first major challenge to sound catechesis in the Universal Church following Vatican II came less than a year after the end of the Council: in October 1966 a book, *De Nieuwe Katechismus,* was published in the Netherlands with an *Imprimatur* from Cardinal Bernard Alfrink, archbishop of Utrecht. This was the since famous "Dutch Catechism", a new catechism commissioned by the hierarchy of the Netherlands and produced by the Higher Catechetical Institute at Nijmegen. It was quickly translated into the major European languages and it almost as quickly became a religious best-seller in most of these languages.

In the United States, the book was published as *A New Catechism: Catholic Faith for Adults.*[2] The very designation of this catechism as being for "adults" was bound to signal something unusual about its contents, just as the same designation in the culture at large serves as a warning about the permissiveness to be found inside. "Christianity is an adult religion", the book jacket proclaimed, and "can be adequately understood and lived only by those who have 'come of age'. It is the child who leads a submissive compliant existence sheltered against the dangers that lurk outside. . . . " The implication was that Catholics were no longer supposed to be "submissive" or "compliant", even though Christ himself had "learned obedience from what he suffered" (Heb 5:8). The tendency of this new catechism thus announced itself before the books' covers were ever opened.

The Dutch Catechism abandoned the traditional question-and-answer catechism format in order to arouse the reader to "think actively about what he reads"; the implication here was that the

[2] *A New Catechism: Catholic Faith for Adults* (New York: Herder and Herder, 1967).

products of the Church's earlier catechisms did *not* think very clearly or deeply about what they read. At the outset, then, this Dutch Catechism exhibited the same condescension and disdain for ordinary Catholics and their traditional formation that had characterized some of the other elements of the catechetical movement that was developing around the same time.

Questions were being raised about this new Dutch Catechism before it was ever published. Ecclesiastical permission to publish it in Germany had been refused, for example. Indeed the various translations were almost all published under various subterfuges. In Germany, for instance, the publisher transferred its rights to the original Dutch publisher to preclude the need for a specific German *Imprimatur;* the first American edition as well simply listed the original Dutch *Imprimatur;* and in France, the book appeared without any *Nihil Obstat* or *Imprimatur* at all (still very unusual for any Catholic book in those days).[3] Similar subterfuges and evasions were to characterize the Dutch Catechism's subsequent publishing career.

Within a month of the Dutch Catechism's appearance, a group of the Catholic laity of Holland petitioned Pope Paul VI to intervene in order to prevent what the group called "great danger for souls" from the Dutch Catechism. Pope Paul VI responded promptly to this petition, asking early in 1967 that three theologians named by the Holy See meet with three theologians selected by the Dutch hierarchy to examine the book. The idea was that the errors, omissions, and distortions that many immediately saw in the Dutch Catechism's treatment of the Catholic faith could be identified and ironed out in a friendly meeting between representatives of Rome as the guardian of the faith and representatives of the new Catechism's principal authors. This hope proved to be entirely illusory; the conference of these six theologians held in northern Italy in April 1967 ended in a total stalemate and

[3] A concise but complete account of the appearance and effects of the Dutch Catechism can be found in Monsignor Eugene Kevane's *Creed and Catechetics* (Westminster, Md.: Christian Classics, 1975). His account is substantially followed here.

sterility; it was a harbinger of similar negative outcomes in subsequent encounters between Roman authority and theologians seeking to function independently of that authority. Two of the theologians on the Dutch side, themselves reputed to be the real "fathers", if not among the principal authors, of the Dutch Catechism itself, were Fathers Edward Schillebeeckx, O.P., and Piet Schoonenberg, S.J., who would be involved in later doctrinal controversies in the years to come. The Dutch side proved to be absolutely adamant in insisting that what had been written in the Dutch Catechism had to stand; this was not to be the last time that proponents of the new catechesis and the new doctrine were to insist that their positions, not those of the Church, henceforth had to be normative in religious education.

With the failure of the conference of the six theologians, Pope Paul VI hastened to name a special commission of cardinals, including some of the giants of of Vatican II, to examine the Dutch Catechism.[4] The pontiff obviously considered this to be a matter of the utmost seriousness: a catechism containing something besides the faith of the Church! The special commission of cardinals first met in June 1967; it appointed a group of theologians from seven different countries to assist in the examination and evaluation of the Dutch Catechism. This work proceeded throughout the summer and fall of 1967. Disputed passages rewritten by the Dutch Catechism's original authors were among the materials examined and rejected. In December 1967 the commission of cardinals met again and identified the doctrinal points and passages that had to be corrected in the Dutch Catechism, providing a statement of the correct basic Catholic doctrine in each instance. It then established a new committee of theologians to compose a new, corrected version of each passage in the Dutch

[4] The commission of cardinals appointed by Pope Paul VI in 1967 to examine the Dutch Catechism included: Cardinal Joseph Frings of Cologne, Cardinal Joseph Lefebvre of Bourges, Cardinal Loren Jaeger of Paderborn, Cardinal Ermengildo Florit of Florence, the Irish Dominican Cardinal Michael Brown of the Roman Curia, and the great Swiss theologian and ecclesiologist Cardinal Charles Journet.

Catechism judged to be deficient. This committee included two of the theologians who had represented the Holy See at the earlier conference of the six theologians, Fathers Edouard Dhanis, S.J., and Jan Visser, C.SS.R. The Dutch bishops' conference designated Monsignor H. J. Fortmann and Father G. Mulders to represent them. The former, Monsignor Fortmann, worked harmoniously with the Holy See's theologians throughout, and he later declared himself to be entirely satisfied with the corrections directed to be made. The latter priest, however, Father Mulders, who belonged to the Catechetical Institute at Nijmegen that had produced the Dutch Catechism in the first place, withdrew in a huff from the committee and not only declined to endorse its results but later publicly protested the corrections that were ordered by the cardinals for the Dutch Catechism.

For the commission of cardinals did indeed order corrections; these corrections were sent to the authors at Nijmegen in March 1968. In June of the same year, the authors of the Dutch Catechism, in one of the first of many defiant gauntlets that would be thrown down before Catholic Church authorities over Catholic doctrine in the next few years, coolly informed the Dutch hierarchy that "we have come to the unequivocal conclusion that the proposed corrections, whether taken singly or as a whole, must be rejected".[5] The authors later issued a *White Book on the New Catechism* explaining "why the corrections for the Catechism prescribed by Rome are unacceptable".[6]

Nevertheless, since the corrections ordered by Rome had indeed been prescribed, and in the midst of worldwide publicity, some editions of the Dutch Catechism were reprinted with the corrections of the cardinals included in the back as an appendix, while the text itself remained the same. This was true of the American edition; the American publisher brought out another edition of *A New Catechism* containing the appendix in a new blue and white jacket to distinguish it from the original edition,

[5] See Kevane, *Creed and Catechetics,* p. 66.

[6] Ibid., p. 281.

which had had a red and white jacket.[7] The text of the Dutch Catechism itself, however, was never corrected, as had been directed by the commission of cardinals. The era of setting aside and ignoring authority in the Church and doing one's own thing instead had begun.

What were the corrections ordered by the commission of cardinals? They are worth summarizing, since they constitute something of an almost prototypical "checklist" of the Catholic doctrines most typically misstated, distorted, or omitted in the religion textbooks of the next couple of decades; they are well worth summarizing here, since anyone concerned with the doctrinal integrity of modern catechesis needs to have them in mind. The corrections ordered for the Dutch Catechism, then, were listed under ten subject headings, as follows:[8]

1. *Points concerning God the Creator.* The commission of cardi-

[7] *A New Catechism: Catholic Faith for Adults* (with Supplement) (New York: Seabury Press, 1969). This book contained an appendix in the back entitled "The Supplement to 'A New Catechism' ", by Edouard Dhanis, S.J., and Jan Visser, C.SS.R., "on behalf of the Commission of Cardinals appointed to examine 'A New Catechism' ". This edition with this Supplement also had an *Imprimatur* dated September 29, 1969, from the Most Reverend Robert F. Joyce, Bishop of Burlington. Perhaps typically, this book, found to be so deficient by the Holy See, carried a laudatory blurb by one of the deans of the catechetical movement in America, Father Gerard S. Sloyan, as follows: "A remarkable synthesis of Christian revelation and human life. Beautifully written and well translated, this volume is in every way a suitable guide to the meaning of Christian life in today's world. It can very well stand as the catechism of the Second Vatican Council." Already so soon after the end of the Council, there was a divorce between the magisterium of the Church and what the "experts" had taken to *calling* "the Christian life" and "the Second Vatican Council"—if there was one thing Vatican II taught it was that any relationship possible with Christ had to come from some degree of membership in his Church, yet the new theologians were prescinding from the Church almost entirely as of little further importance.

[8] A final Declaration on "A New Catechism" was issued by the papal commission of cardinals on October 15, 1968, and is reprinted in Kevane, *Creed and Catechetics,* pp. 181–89; it contains the corrections ordered by the cardinals under ten headings.

nals required that the Dutch Catechism teach that God, "besides this sensible world in which we live, has created also a realm of pure spirits whom we call angels". (This is an interesting point considering the attitude toward angels to be taken over two decades later by some of the authors of *The Universal Catechism Reader.*) The commission also specified that the Dutch Catechism should "state explicitly that individual human souls, since they are spiritual, are created immediately by God".

2. *The Fall of Man in Adam.* Explicit mention was required of the Catholic teaching that "man in the beginning of history rebelled against God, and so lost for himself and his offspring that sanctity and justice in which he had been constituted".

3. *The Conception of Jesus by the Virgin Mary.* The commission of cardinals asked that the Dutch Catechism "openly profess that the Blessed Mother of the Incarnate Word always enjoyed the honor of virginity".

4. *The "Satisfaction" Made by Christ Our Lord.* The commission directed that "the essential elements of the doctrine of the satisfaction of Christ which pertains to our faith are to be proposed without ambiguity".

5. *The Sacrifice of the Cross and the Sacrifice of the Mass.* The cardinals directed that it be "clearly stated that Jesus offered Himself to His Father to repair our wrong-doing as a holy victim in whom God was well pleased.... The sacrifice of the Cross is perpetuated in the Church of God as the eucharistic sacrifice."

6. *The Eucharistic Presence and the Eucharistic Change.* The commission of cardinals declared on this subject: "It is necessary that in the text of the Catechism it be brought out beyond doubt that after the consecration of the bread and wine the very body and blood of Christ is present on the altar and is received sacramentally in Holy Communion... a conversion which in the Church is termed transubstantiation.... "

7. *The Infallibility of the Church and the Knowledge of Revealed Mysteries.* Under this heading the Dutch catechism was required to state clearly "that the infallibility of the Church does not give

her only a safe course in a continual research, but the truth in maintaining the doctrine of the faith and explaining it always in the same sense".

8. *The Ministerial or Hierarchical Priesthood and the Power of Teaching in the Church.* The commission of cardinals required under this heading that care be taken "not to minimize the excellence of the ministerial priesthood, that in its participation in the priesthood of Christ, it differs from the common priesthood of the faithful, not only in degree, but in essence." Under the same heading, the Dutch Catechism was required to state that "the teaching authority and power of ruling in the Church is given directly to the Holy Father and the bishops joined to him in hierarchical communion"—and not, in other words, to the People of God first.

9. *Various Points concerning Dogmatic Theology.* Under this heading the Dutch Catechism was to be corrected to affirm certain points about the contemplation of the Trinity, the efficacy of the sacraments, and the souls of the just in purgatory.

10. *Certain Points of Moral Theology.* Finally, the commission of cardinals wanted the Dutch Catechism to affirm "the existence of moral laws which we are able to know and express in such wise that they bind our consciences always and in all circumstances"—here again, the problem foreshadowed a perennial one in the thinking of some Catholics since Vatican II; the same problem would recur in *The Universal Catechism Reader* more than two decades later. The Dutch Catechism was also directed under this heading to include a presentation of the Church's full teaching on conjugal morality, including the indissolubility of marriage—another perennial problem.

These, then, were the ten points in the Dutch Catechism that required correction, according to the special commission of cardinals appointed by Pope Paul VI to examine this strange new production commissioned by the Dutch hierarchy. These ten points constitute practically a summary of some of the major doctrinal errors of the present day; they would appear in many places in the ensuing years, especially in some of the new religion textbooks.[9] The Dutch Catechism was unusually influential, as a matter of fact, and it helped diffuse quite widely the same errors, distortions, and omissions identified in it by the commission of cardinals. All this was in accordance with the psychology familiar from the cases of books or movies that become popular *because* someone tried to "censor" them.

2.

The whole Dutch Catechism affair in all its various aspects—authorship by prestigious theologians not only not respectful of the magisterium of the Church but consciously asserting their independence and autonomy from it; sponsorship of the resulting religious ambiguity if not outright error both by those in high places in the Church and also in the groves of academe; insistence that the Church's faith must henceforth be judged by scholarly, worldly, and even pragmatic standards; open defiance of Church authority attempting to correct distortions, omissions, or errors in doctrine; recourse to the public media in order to try to influence the Catholic faithful to line up on the side of those challenging Church authority, considered now "behind the times"—all these things were to become regular features of the life of the Church over the next two decades and more. The ancient notion of *Roma locuta est, causa finita est* was simply to become inoperative, if it had not already been so by the time of the Dutch Catechism affair. Henceforth theologians and experts were to be the ones who would decide what was Catholic and what was not, or at any rate they were certainly to have a say equal to that of the pope and the

[9] See *Our New Catechisms: A Critical Analysis* (New Rochelle, N.Y.: Catholics United for the Faith, December 8, 1970). This booklet analyzed four of the most typical and commonly used of the new religion textbook series in America using the ten doctrinal points identified by the commission of cardinals examining the Dutch Catechism. The textbook series published by W. H. Sadlier, Inc., Benziger Brothers, Allyn and Bacon, and the Paulist Press were all found to contain some errors, distortions, and omissions on many of these same points.

bishops in the matter. This state of affairs was taken for granted by the time the critics of the provisional text of the Catechism for the Universal Church came along in 1990.

It is important to underline, however, that Pope Paul VI treated the Dutch Catechism affair as a major crisis of faith; ecclesiastical authority *tried* to deal with the situation at the time, even if its efforts to do so did not bear the hoped-for fruit. For Pope Paul VI, a situation where established theologians could write a "catechism" containing as all-pervasive a pattern of doctrinal error as the Dutch Catechism did could hardly be accidental; the fact that the whole production was actually sponsored by a national hierarchy, tranquilly letting such errors pass and even, in a sense, defending them (or at least letting the Catechism's authors get away with defying Rome), only made the situation worse. These theologians could not have been ignorant of what the Church taught, and had always taught, on the ten points identified by the commission of cardinals, nor could the bishops of the Netherlands have been ignorant of it; the problem was not that they did not know, but that they did not believe the Catholic faith in its fullness and integrity, as handed down from the apostles and authentically interpreted by the magisterium of the Church. It was clearly a crisis of faith, and the Pope saw it clearly.

Even as he was naming Dutch theologians loyal to the Holy See to meet with representatives of the Dutch hierarchy, Pope Paul VI, in February 1967, was also preparing to proclaim what he was to call a "Year of Faith". If the faith was in crisis and at risk, it followed that it needed to be reaffirmed. The occasion was the nineteenth centenary of the martyrdom of the holy apostles Peter and Paul; both had been martyred in Rome sometime between 64 and 68 A.D., during the persecutions under the emperor Nero. While it was impossible to fix the exact date of their martyrdom, Pope Pius IX had celebrated the eighteenth centenary of the event in 1867, one hundred years earlier. Hence Paul VI selected 1967 for his celebration; the principal event of this celebration was to take place on the liturgical feast for the martyrdom of Saints Peter and Paul; the Church celebrates this on June 29th.

However, in addition to a celebration to coincide with the one Pius IX had held a century earlier, Pope Paul VI also decreed a special commemoration that was to last an entire year: from June 29, 1967, to June 29, 1968. This was Paul VI's "Year of Faith". The Pontiff hoped

> that the commemorative centenary of the martyrdom of SS. Peter and Paul will find its expression chiefly in a great act of faith throughout the Church. We want to see this anniversary as a providential occasion given to the People of God for re-awakening a fuller awareness of its faith, giving it fresh life, purifying it, strengthening it, and giving testimony to it. We cannot fail to know that the present time shows there is a great need of this.

In particular, Paul VI wanted sustained attention paid to what he called "the meaning of the Creed": if elements of the Creed were what was being denied, then these same elements needed to be reaffirmed again in a special way.

In connection with this attempt to reaffirm those elements of the faith being particularly challenged by modern assumptions, Paul VI made a special appeal to "those engaged in the study of sacred Scripture and theology, to collaborate with the hierarchical teaching authority of the Church in defending the faith from all error . . . in correctly expounding its content, and in drawing up reasoned norms for its study and spread. This same appeal we make to preachers, to teachers of religion, and to catechists. . . ."[10]

Why all this extraordinary attention given to the subject of the faith itself? Because, as the Pope saw it, the faith was in crisis; the faith was in danger. One of the strongest proofs of this was the affair of the Dutch Catechism; it was not the only proof, but it was one of them. Pope Paul VI was no naïve romantic, urging a

[10] Pope Paul VI, Apostolic Exhortation Announcing the Year of Faith, February 22, 1967, reprinted *in toto* in Kevane, *Creed and Catechetics,* pp. 164–70.

sentimental devotion to faith; he was a hard-headed realist trying to get people's attention; he was discerning the *real* "signs of the times", namely, that the corrosive acids of modernity were eating away at the heart of the faith from the inside. More than two decades later, there appear to be some who have not yet noticed, or at any rate have not yet admitted, what Paul VI was trying to remedy back in 1967.

In his exhortation announcing the Year of Faith, Pope Paul VI carefully and explicitly listed the things that, in his view, constituted the principal dangers to the faith; these dangers resided especially in the fact that

> ... new opinions in exegesis and theology often borrowed from bold but blind secular philosophies have in places found a way into the realm of Catholic teaching. They question or distort the objective sense of truths taught with authority by the Church; under the pretext of adapting religious thought to the contemporary outlook, they prescind from the guidance of the Church's teaching, give the foundations of theological speculation a direction of historicism, dare to rob Holy Scripture's testimony of its sacred and historical character, and try to introduce a so-called "postconciliar" mentality among the People of God; this neglects the solidity and consistency of the Council's vast and magnificent developments of teaching and legislation, neglects with it the Church's accumulated riches of thought and practice in order to overturn the spirit of traditional fidelity and spread about the illusion of giving Christianity a new interpretation, which is arbitrary and barren. What would remain of the content of our faith, or of the theological virtue that professes it, if these attempts, freed from the support of the Church's teaching authority, were destined to prevail?[11]

What indeed? Paul VI provided a pretty accurate description of the state of mind that produced the Dutch Catechism; it is not a bad description of the state of mind that produced *The Universal Catechism Reader* for that matter. What the Dutch Catechism managed to undermine and erode was bad enough; it would have

[11] Ibid., pp. 168–69.

been that much worse if Paul VI had allowed it to spread its errors throughout the whole Church, unchecked and unchallenged.

But the Pope went even farther. At the end of his Year of Faith proclaimed in order to try to get Catholics to focus more sharply on the dangers to the faith, thereby affirming it more positively, "giving it fresh life, purifying it, strengthening it, and giving testimony to it", the Pope did something even more extraordinary. In fulfillment of what he called his "duty to fulfill the mandate given by Christ to Peter", Pope Paul VI went on to provide nothing less than a comprehensive restatement of the faith for modern times. On June 30, 1968, at the closing of his Year of Faith, Paul VI solemnly proclaimed a Profession of Faith—what has come to be known as his Credo of the People of God. This Credo was in the form of the classic Catholic Church Creed, variations of which have been issued on various occasions in the history of the Church, the best-known examples being the Nicene Creed recited every Sunday at Mass by all the faithful and the familiar Apostles' Creed recited, for example, at the beginning of every Rosary.

In content Pope Paul VI's Credo of the People of God followed the general outline familiar from the Nicene and other Creeds. In restating the basic faith of the Church, though, Paul VI paid particular attention to those points of doctrine or elements of the Creed subject to doubt or under attack today; these particular points the Pope often elaborated on, paying careful attention to detail, in order to reaffirm them in the face of the modern challenges to them. This elaboration and reaffirmation of controverted elements of the Church's faith is what makes Paul VI's Credo of the People of God distinctive. For example, the Pope went out of his way to reassert the Church's belief in those spiritual beings created by God called angels (as was noted in Chapter 1 of the present study).

Similarly, Paul VI went on at length on the subject of original sin, even directly quoting the Council of Trent on the subject, as was quoted in Chapter 2. The Pope insisted on using the term "transubstantiation"; he reaffirmed the reality of death, judgment, heaven, and hell. A careful reading of the Credo of the People of God would yield a virtual reaffirmation of all the ten points that the cardinals found had to be corrected in the Dutch Catechism, although the Credo was intended to be a positive restatement of the Church's faith and not just a refutation of Dutch errors.

Pope Paul VI's Credo of the People of God is in print in many editions, is included in many collections of Church documents, and is easily available to any loyal Catholic or serious inquirer; it need not therefore be printed here *in toto.* What is important about it is that the Pope saw fit to issue such a document at all in the situation in which he found himself when the crisis in the Church's faith became apparent to him. He issued it, he said at the time, because he wanted to "confirm our brothers in the faith"; he also did so, he added, because of

> ... the disquiet which agitates certain modern quarters with regard to the faith. They do not escape the influence of a world being profoundly changed, in which so many certainties are being disputed or discussed. We see even Catholics allowing themselves to be seized by a kind of passion for change and novelty.... [12]

Pope Paul VI disclaimed any intention of making any kind of "dogmatic definition" in his Credo of the People of God.[13] Yet the fact that the Supreme Pastor of the Church would go to the trouble, after an intensive, year-long buildup, to proclaim solemnly to the whole world a comprehensive restatement of what the Catholic fundamentally believes, surely points to the fact that the Pope was quite serious about it all; the Credo surely represents and was intended to represent authentic, binding Catholic teaching of the type that Vatican II said had to be adhered to by Catholics with a "loyal submission of the will and intellect ... even when [the pope] does not speak *ex cathedra*".[14]

Yet, as became clear in connection with the discussion about

[12] Pope Paul VI, Introduction to the Credo of the People of God.

[13] Ibid.

[14] Vatican Council II, *Lumen Gentium,* no. 25.

the existence of angels in Chapter 1, the Credo of the People of God, since its issuance, has not always been treated by Catholic theologians as an authentic statement of the magisterium of the Church; it has often been treated, rather, as a mere statement of theological opinion, outdated theological opinion at that. Citing it has not settled many arguments; indeed many arguments are conducted as if the document had never been issued at all; it has been one of the quickest of all modern Church documents to have been consigned down the memory hole.

But what this indicates is that the crisis of faith perceived by Pope Paul VI had already gone too far before the document was issued for its issuance to have had the desired effect in helping arrest the erosion of the faith; already by the time the Credo of the People of God was issued, many theologians were no longer interested in what the supreme authority in the Church might decide on the level of ordinary teaching; these theologians had already reached the conclusion that the ordinary teachings of the Church could safely be left aside when "good" reasons existed for doing so; the supreme, though ordinary, teaching of the Vicar of Christ was no longer of any special importance—but this is merely another way of saying that there was indeed a crisis of faith: faith in the Church and her magisterium and the assistance it receives from the Holy Spirit.

An editorial in *Commonweal* magazine that immediately greeted the Credo of the People of God seemed to have been written expressly to demonstrate that the Pope had been only too right in discerning the existence of a serious crisis of faith in the Church, particularly among theologians and scholars. "Almost single-handedly, Pope Paul has tried to keep the lingering vestiges of ultramontanism alive", *Commonweal* averred. "Most signs point in one direction", this editorial continued. "He is failing. Where the pressures against the papacy in the nineteenth century were primarily external, now they are primarily internal"—meaning that the new theologians, the Dutch catechists, and people like the *Commonweal* editorial writer had no intention of submitting any longer to Church authority in the old way that the Church, however, had not ceased to affirm was necessary in order to be a Catholic in the full sense of the word. How far the modern crisis of faith had progressed not even Paul VI had realized; but the *Commonweal* editorial on his Credo made it perfectly clear:

> There cannot be many Catholic biblical theologians left who would be willing to speak of an "original offense" committed by someone named "Adam." There cannot be many sacramental theologians left who would say that the doctrine of the real presence is "very appropriately called by the Church transubstantiation." There cannot be many liturgists around to glorify adoration of the "Blessed Host." There cannot be many ecclesiologists left who would give the biblical image of the Church as "Body of Christ" primacy over other images. There cannot be many dogmatic theologians left who would care to speak of those who refuse God's love and pity as "going to the fire that will not extinguish." In sum, there cannot be many theologians left who would be able to assent to a message and a "new Credo" whose content not only fails to reflect even Vatican II, but even more fails to admit what has happened to theology since then.[15]

It should be noted that "what has happened to theology" seems to be the main point here; theology is now apparently determinative of faith, not vice versa. The content of the Catholic faith is apparently something that is henceforth to be decided by "biblical theologians", "sacramental theologians", "liturgists", "ecclesiologists", "dogmatic theologians", and other such assorted experts. What the pope and the bishops might have to say about all this is apparently of interest only to the extent that it is endorsed or adopted by these theologians and experts.

Reading over such an editorial as this makes one wonder how anyone reading it without immediately reacting to it as egregiously wrong could any longer even be considered Catholic in the full sense of the word. Yet the thing was written over twenty years ago, and *Commonweal* magazine has gone merrily on since then,

[15] Editorial, "The Pope's New 'Credo' ", in *Commonweal,* July 12, 1968.

presumably not lacking for readers who do consider themselves Catholic. Nevertheless the fact that such an editorial could even be written, much less accepted by educated Catholic readers, bespeaks a momentous departure from the meaning of the Catholic faith as it has been commonly understood down through history until the present day. Pope Paul VI was absolutely on target in discerning a grave crisis of faith in all this.

It should be remembered that the entire episode of the Dutch Catechism, the efforts of the commission of cardinals, the Year of Faith, and the Credo of the People of God—followed by a scandalous defiance of every effort of Church authority to state or correct her authentic faith—all occurred prior to the issuance of Pope Paul VI's 1968 encyclical *Humanae Vitae* reiterating the Church's teaching against artificial birth control. The massive rejection of that encyclical, both inside and outside the Church, confirmed that a new mentality had indeed installed itself within the Church; Catholics could no longer be counted on to accept the teachings of the Church as expounded by the magisterium. This was a novel thing in the Church and planted seeds of radical doubt: if the Church did not speak for Christ on birth control, perhaps there was a host of other issues on which she did not speak for him either. Even before *Humanae Vitae* had appeared, however, the reception accorded to Pope Paul VI's Credo of the People of God had already signaled the new era of radical doubt in the Church. There was no way that religious education could remain unaffected by the new climate, and it was not.

3.

Pope Paul VI moved to issue his Credo of the People of God as soon as it became clear to him from the Dutch Catechism episode and similar episodes how radically and extensively the faith was being questioned by some of the Church's own sons and daughters. The crisis of faith he was so concerned about might have been equally clear to him if he had looked at the rapid adoption of anthropocentric and experiential catechesis by the catechetical movement, for example, or if he had noted the determination of some religious educators to become autonomous professionals instead of seeing their task primarily as one of serving Christ in the Church.

One of the great mysteries of the postconciliar era, however, is the number of Catholics who apparently do not see that there is any crisis of faith. Part of the explanation for this may be that heterodox statements by Catholics may have become so commonplace that nobody remarks on them any longer; they have lost their shock value; the sharp edges that authentic Catholic faith should have have become dulled and blunted in the present climate. If the Church teaches theological opinion and not saving truth, then why *not* counter the Church's opinion with one's own opinion?

Cardinal John O'Connor of New York well articulated the dilemma faced in the present sceptical and permissive climate by anybody commissioned to teach in the Church today, at whatever level. Speaking at a meeting in Rome between American archbishops and Pope John Paul II, Cardinal O'Connor declared:

> I believe that circumstances surrounding the publication of *Humanae Vitae* seriously eroded the credibility of Church teaching. I am not for a moment questioning the validity of *Humanae Vitae.* I am saying that when Catholics learned—and it took them no time at all—that they could shop around among confessors for opinions on birth control, they soon decided that they didn't have to confess the matter at all. In my judgment, we have not yet recovered from this confusion. One gets a sense that a kind of moral free-enterprise system took over at some point. The "moral market" has been allowed to float.[16]

The basic dilemma here is quite clear. What may not have been quite so clear is how regularly and diligently Church authority has moved to reassert the claims of the magisterium and reiterate

[16] Cardinal John O'Connor, "The Bishop as Teacher of the Faith", in *Origins,* NC Documentary Service, March 23, 1989.

correct teaching, just as Pope Paul VI moved so quickly to reaffirm the faith of the Church in the Credo of the People of God. The reason it is not always appreciated how frequently and persistently the Church has moved to reiterate her correct faith is that the reiteration is too frequently treated in the way the original doctrine was: it is set aside, whether or not it is formally denied.

In the field of religious education, all things considered, the Church has similarly moved with reasonable promptitude to state her correct faith as against today's regular challenges to it. The *General Catechetical Directory,* for example, was issued on April 11, 1971, less than six years after the Vatican II Decree on the Pastoral Office of Bishops in the Church that mandated this particular document.[17] This is a relatively brief period, considering that the GCD, like so many other Church documents, was drafted by the familiar international committee of, in this case, priests and bishops; it had to go out to the national conferences of bishops for comments; and, finally, it had to be reviewed by a mixed commission from the two Congregations for the Clergy and for the Doctrine of the Faith.[18]

Moreover, the GCD, when issued, turned out to be a very "doctrinal" and orthodox document; it very much served the purpose of reaffirming the importance of doctrine and cognitive learning of the faith at a time when these things had gone out of fashion in the catechetical movement. For it certainly remains true that many who wanted a "directory" instead of a "catechism" wanted it *because* doctrine had already come to be considered less important in catechesis, and so they did not want anything as definite as a catechism that, by definition, would restate doctrine.

No matter how doctrinal and orthodox the GCD was, however, the religious education establishment was nevertheless all ready

[17] Vatican Council II, *Christus Dominus,* no. 44.

[18] See Father Berard Marthaler, "The Genesis and Genius of the *General Catechetical Directory*", in Michael Warren, ed., *Sourcebook for Modern Catechetics* (Winona, Minn.: St. Mary's Press, 1983), p. 251. The only American on the international commission of experts responsible for preparing the GCD was Monsignor Russell Neighbor.

for it when it came out; it had to be assimilated into the existing system, and therefore it was seen as a great boon simply because it was not a catechism. For Father Berard Marthaler, a perennial leader in both the catechetical movement and the religious education establishment, the GCD "symbolize[d] the move away from the chimera of a universal catechism". According to this same author (who, as already noted, would also turn up years later as one of the authors of *The Universal Catechism Reader*), the GCD also meant "another step away from book-centered catechesis by twice stating that the role of catechists is more important than texts".[19] This, of course, is entirely true, though the GCD always assumes that what these catechists are transmitting is the authentic faith of the Church as expounded by the magisterium, not some species of modern theology or theory of social justice. Indeed, the second of two references made by Father Marthaler to the GCD specifies, precisely, that catechists must be "rightly formed" (GCD, no. 108), and it can be pretty safely affirmed that no catechist trained exclusively in "anthropocentric" or "experiential" catechesis can be said to be "rightly formed" according to the GCD's own standards.

In any event, those inclined to prefer a directory instead of a catechism in order to avoid the emphasis on doctrine were not obliged by the Holy See. The GCD itself possesses a strong doctrinal chapter 2 (nos. 38–55), with the title "The More Outstanding Elements of the Christian Message", in which the tenets of the Catholic faith are stated with a precision and exactitude that would surely merit the scorn of another *Commonweal* editorial. Moreover, the GCD in no way downgrades catechisms but rather declares that "the greatest importance must be attached to catechisms published by ecclesiastical authority", the reason for this being that these official catechisms "provide under a form that is condensed and practical the witnesses of revelation and of Christian tradition" (GCD, no. 119). Nor does the GCD abandon trying to teach the faith by addressing doctrinal propositions

[19] Ibid., p. 253.

expressing it to the mind rather than relying on experience or assimilation of some vague kind of Christian "good feeling". Rather, echoing Vatican II's *Christus Dominus,* no. 14 (without excluding preaching and liturgical forms of catechesis), the GCD flatly declares that the intention of catechesis is nothing else but "to make men's faith becoming living, conscious, and active through the light of *instruction*" (GCD, no. 17; emphasis added). Finally, the GCD made clear that catechesis is indeed an ecclesial affair that has to do with transmitting the faith of Christ to believers, whole and entire:

> Since the purpose of catechesis . . . consists in leading individual Christians and communities to a mature faith, it must take diligent care faithfully to present the entire treasure of the Christian message. This must surely be done according to the divine pedagogy, but with the full store of revelation that has been divinely communicated being taken into account, so that the People of God may be nourished by it and live from it.
>
> Catechesis begins, therefore, with a rather simple presentation of the entire structure of the Christian message (using also summary or global formulas), and it presents this in a way appropriate to the various cultural and spiritual conditions of those to be taught. By no means, however, can it stop with this first presentation, but it must be interested in presenting the content in an always more detailed and developed manner. . . .
>
> This task of catechesis, not an easy one, must be carried out under the guidance of the magisterium of the Church, whose duty it is to safeguard the truth of the divine message, and to watch that the ministry uses appropriate forms of speaking (GCD, no. 38).

Thus the *General Catechetical Directory.* It can safely be affirmed that, if this single passage had always been understood and observed, there would have been no crisis in catechesis in the postconciliar era. Yet the above short paragraphs constitute only one small part of an otherwise very rich and useful document. The GCD, in short, is an excellent guide for anyone who will consent to be guided by it; it is one of the finest things to emerge out of Vatican II.

Yet, as has already been noted in Chapter 1, the undisputed reign of the GCD as the Church's primary guide for the teaching of religion was destined to last only for a relatively brief period of time—from the time the document was promulgated in 1971 until the 1985 Synod of Bishops when it was proposed and decided that the Church should return to the basic kind of universal catechism that had once been the assumed norm in the Church but that had been passed over by Vatican II.

The reasons why the Synod of Bishops believed it was necessary to go back to an actual catechism had little to do with the GCD itself. The GCD was fine, entirely suited to the purpose for which it was designed. The trouble was not with the GCD but with the way the GCD was received and implemented by a religious education establishment indoctrinated into the ideas of the modern catechetical movement and the new theology, the new liturgy, the new exegesis, and so on. Or rather: the trouble was with the way in which the GCD was *not* implemented by the religious education establishment, for the GCD turned out to be one of those Church documents that was never "received" by those who should have been most directly involved in its proper implementation, namely, the new catechists.

4.

The religious education establishment, at least in the United States, received the *General Catechetical Directory* with an outward show of respect; there was no open rebellion nor overt signs of defiance when it came out; on the contrary, there was talk as if the thing were actually going to be used and observed. This was a necessary stance. The American hierarchy was not disposed to allow the same degree of open defiance of Roman judgments that the Dutch hierarchy had been willing to countenance in the case of the Dutch Catechism. Sensing this, American religious educators have generally worked hard at presenting themselves as loyal to their bishops; they generally go along to get along. Besides, the practical autonomy they have generally enjoyed in their own sphere has often allowed them to do pretty much as they pleased in practice while presenting themselves as in accord, for example, with the GCD.

There did arise, though, at least one crisis churned up in part at least by the appearance of the GCD. This was the matter of First Confession/First Communion. In accordance with fashionable psychological theories, many American dioceses had been following the practice on an experimental basis of administering First Communion to young children before they had made their First Confession. The GCD, however, contained an appendix that had the effect of restoring the earlier discipline that had originally been established by Pope Saint Pius X, namely First Confession before First Communion.

Hence there was considerable resistance in America to what was seen as one more onerous new Roman imposition, although it had been the regular practice within everyone's living memory, and Rome was actually "imposing" less than ever; but the American religious education establishment was by this time well indoctrinated in the new thinking and therefore was not disposed to go along with anything as traditional as First Confession before First Communion. The idea was that children that young could not really commit sin serious enough to require confession; the pedagogy of the traditional practice appeared to have been lost on these professional pedagogues anyway. The director of religious education of the Brooklyn diocese, for example, Father Howard Basler, saw the whole thing as nothing else but an exercise of "ecclesiastical power" on account of which it was necessary "to talk back to the perpetrators of the affront",[20] meaning the pope and the Congregation for the Clergy then headed by the American Cardinal Wright. This reaction was all too typical. The whole spirit of resistance indicated here typified exactly what Rome had encountered in trying to get the errors in the Dutch Catechism corrected.

[20] Quoted in Monsignor George A. Kelly, *Keeping the Church Catholic with John Paul II* (New York: Doubleday, 1990), p. 66.

The controversy over First Confession/First Communion raged on for years and has probably not been really satisfactorily resolved to this day. The Church's discipline remains what it is; Canon 914 of the new 1983 Code of Canon Law prescribes communion as early as possible after the onset of the age of reason, "preceded by sacramental confession". One has an impression (very unscientific) that the situation has improved since the new Code of Canon Law came into effect, and that many if not most American dioceses now follow the correct practice; at any rate the controversy over the whole thing died down, and most of the participants went on to other things.

Aside from the First Confession/First Communion conflict, there was no open revolt against the *General Catechetical Directory.* Nevertheless it was only received by the American religious education establishment after a statement had been secured at the 1971 International Catechetical Congress in Rome, as already noted in Chapter 2, to the effect that the GCD was a "service document" and not binding "legislation".[21] This statement by itself had the practical effect of converting the GCD into something that everyone could interpret in his own fashion; and "service", of course, has always been as big a word in the postconciliar vocabulary as "legislation" and "binding" have not. What it meant was that, in practice, the GCD was to be yet another directory that did not really "direct", a guidebook that did not really "guide". Lip service would readily be paid to this Roman document; but the religious educators would go on exactly as before.

This became clear quite soon. The GCD became available in an authorized English translation only in December 1971.[22] By September 1972, the religious education establishment had produced its own "commentary" on the document, setting forth its own idea of what the GCD really said and required, for the instruction of Catholic religious educators in the United States. This com-

[21] "Final and Approved Resolutions of the English-speaking Language Group", International Catechetical Congress, September 1971, in Warren, ed., *Sourcebook,* p. 81.

[22] Berard Marthaler, "Modern Catechetical Movement", p. 256.

mentary was a small book with the title *Focus on American Catechetics.*[23] According to its subtitle, it was "A Commentary on the General Catechetical Directory". This little book was published by the National Conference of Diocesan Directors of Religious Education (NCDDRE), the association of directors, associate directors, and assistant directors of religious education in U.S. dioceses, affiliated with the National Catholic Education Association (NCEA). It was authored by Fathers Thomas F. Sullivan and John F. Meyers, the then NCDDRE president and executive secretary, respectively.

Henceforth there was to be, therefore, what could only be considered a quasi-official commentary on the GCD that, in cases of doubt or dispute, could always be safely followed by American religious educators instead of the GCD itself. Why a document as relatively short, clear, and concise as the GCD needed a "commentary" at all was another question. Whether or not there was a need for one, *Focus on American Catechetics* was produced.

Focus begins by trying to insure that the GCD would be seen by American Catholic religious educators not only as not binding "legislation" but as a document actually reflecting their own ideas and concerns and providing a green light for just about everything that was already going on in religious education. The GCD "not only evidences a keen sensibility to various theological viewpoints", the preface to *Focus* asserts, "but insists that the application of its admittedly general principles and directives is the prerogative of the national conferences of bishops",[24] in other words, in practice, of the religious educators themselves in place. The phrase "theological viewpoints" was already by then long since established as a code phrase pertaining not to theology, strictly taken, at all, but to variant versions of the Catholic faith itself that various freewheeling theologians of the day were busily outlining; the religious educators, by and large, were the eager disciples of the new

[23] Revs. Thomas F. Sullivan and John F. Meyers, *Focus on American Catechetics: A Commentary on the General Catechetical Directory* (Washington, D.C.: NCEA National Conference of Diocesan Directors of Religious Education, 1972).

[24] Ibid., p. iii and p. 3.

theologians, and hence they needed an interpretation of the GCD that would allow these kinds of ideas to be presented in catechesis as developments of the faith. For the GCD, of course, in no way countenanced anything like this; nor had the idea of doing so probably ever entered the minds of its authors, who assumed the unity of the authentic faith that the GCD in fact reflects.

The authors of *Focus* found it "puzzling" that the GCD in its foreword should refer to doctrines that are "to be held by all". After all, the GCD was not supposed to be "legislation". However, authentic Catholic doctrines *are* "to be held by all" in the nature of the case (see *Lumen Gentium,* no. 25) and not just because the GCD mentions it in passing. The GCD did not have to legislate any such thing because it was already required by the Church and would have been required by the Church if the GCD had never been written. The comment by the authors of *Focus* is all too symptomatic of the new catechetical outlook that appears to be that nobody has to believe anything pertaining to the Catholic faith any longer that is not specifically and expressly "legislated"; otherwise everything is up for grabs and can be manipulated by the new theologians and the new catechists as they wish. Since the GCD itself had been established not to be "legislation", it had no business speaking about any such things as doctrine "to be held by all". Presumably only a modern religious educator could have moved far enough away from the traditional faith as to imagine that the GCD was saying anything new here.

In format and layout, *Focus on American Catechetics* consists of brief summaries of the contents of the GCD, followed by its own comments on it. The summaries are for the most part straightforward and accurate; it is in the comments that the imagination of the authors is allowed free rein. *Focus* dares at times to be openly and bluntly critical of the GCD. For example, on page 63, it calls GCD no. 38's requirement that catechesis begin with a presentation "of the entire structure of the Christian message" to be "educational nonsense" at which American teachers can only "cringe". The comment reflects the actual American situation, where "the entire structure of the Christian message" sometimes failed to get conveyed throughout the entire length of catechesis, kindergarten through grade twelve, not just at the beginning.

For the most part, though, the plan of the authors of *Focus* appears to have been to proceed by indirection. The text usually does not directly contradict what the GCD says; it simply shifts the typical GCD focus and puts it into the desired context of current American catechetical practice. Thus on the subject of revelation on page 22, *Focus* grants GCD no. 10's assertion that faith is a gift of God whereby man accepts divine revelation, but then goes on on the next page to assert, contrary to the GCD, that there are actually two types of revelation: "The first view, with which many will be familiar from their childhood training, sees revelation as a body of doctrine or truths revealed to us by God." Vatican II, of course, similarly taught that a revelation handed down from the time of the apostles in the Church necessarily has to do primarily with the message, or truths, thus transmitted, namely, "the mystery of his will" (Vatican II, *Dei Verbum,* no. 2). Suddenly however, all this is nothing but a "view", one, moreover, mostly "familiar from . . . childhood", and no doubt now to be faintly belittled by sophisticated adults. Yet this view "familiar from . . . childhood training" is precisely what some religious educators do not want passed on to the students; thus, this view of revelation will *not* be familiar from the childhood training of the next generation. This is a pity, because it also happens to be the Church's view of revelation.

Focus proceeds (p. 23): "Another view of revelation and faith has become more prominent in the Church, at least since the time of Vatican II. It looks at revelation as a process in which God primarily communicates Himself and not just data about Himself and His plan for us. It is a more personalistic approach and sees man's participation in this loving communion as integral to the notion of revelation." Properly understood and as far as it goes, this is not wrong—although the use of the word "process" does conceal a very deep pit that can quite easily be fallen into. But as Pope John Paul II himself teaches in *Catechesi Tradendae,* for example: "At the heart of catechesis we find, in essence, a Person, the Person of Jesus of Nazareth . . . [Catholic] teaching is not a body of abstract truths. It is the communication of the living mystery of God."[25]

In view of the fact that ultimate Christian truth resides in a person, the real problem for religious education is therefore continually to communicate Christ, "the image of the invisible God" (Col 1:15). This is one of the main reasons that GCD no. 40 specifies that "catechesis must necessarily be Christocentric"; but since Christ was taken up into heaven on Ascension Thursday nearly two thousand years ago, it is also necessary to communicate him as GCD no. 17 says—as has already been quoted—namely, "through the light of instruction". This instruction is strictly necessary, and must also include all the truths of the whole message that Christ came into the world, *inter alia,* to preach and teach, which the apostles received and handed down; and which the Catholic Church professes and authentically interprets through her living magisterium. If all these truths are properly and consistently communicated to the mind of the catechumens, they will, with the help of grace and the sacraments, truly develop a "living, conscious, and active" faith: it will be "personalistic" and it will involve a "loving communion". Moreover, it is the point of catechesis.

Focus and its NCDDRE authors, though, on page 24, downgrade the importance of this absolutely necessary kind of instruction by characterizing it as concern "about the exactitude of verbal formulas"; they then go on to say:

> On the other hand, if the educator views revelation in more dynamic and personal terms, he will seek to become conscious of the signs of the living God present in their own lives. He will not see his task as primarily transmitting unspoiled doctrines from the deep freeze of the past, but rather as helping the student reflect on his own experience. He will begin from the experience of the student and will provide real and vicarious experiences upon which the student can reflect. His religion

[25] *Catechesi Tradendae,* nos. 5 and 7.

classes will be characterized by creative, integrating activities (pp. 24–25).

The first and most obvious thing to be said about this approach is that it is most certainly not "Christocentric", as specified by GCD, no. 40; it is "student-o-centric". It is focused on the student and his psychology. It is also, and necessarily, anti-content; indeed, it is anti-truth ("unspoiled doctrines from the deep-freeze of the past"). "Helping the student reflect on his own experience" cannot possibly lead to faith by itself. Christ's life and message have to be put before the student in words addressed to the student's mind if the faith in Christ implanted by baptism is ever to take root and grow. "Faith, then, comes through hearing, and what is heard is the word of Christ" (Rom 10:17). Trying to "provide real and vicarious experiences" that truly relate to Christ and his salvific message will mostly be as inane and vacuous as so many of the modern religion textbooks and religious education materials have in fact turned out to be. There will not *be* any "signs of the living God present" in the lives of students if they are not steadily taught the truths about God as his Church professes and proclaims them.

Focus claims on page 27 that its view of revelation requiring recourse to the experiential method is consistent with the GCD, which, according to *Focus,* does not "impose" what is called "a single theology" on catechesis. In reality, however, this so-called commentary on the GCD is really working quite patently at cross-purposes with it.

Focus on American Catechetics thus integrally reflects the creedless, contentless, almost exclusively anthropocentric, and experiential catechesis already long in vogue in the catechetical movement and thus favored by the religious education establishment in the United States. What this means is that this commentary on the GCD simply interprets that document in a way that fits these views, since in no way does the GCD propose or promote or even allow the kind of new catechesis that *Focus* represents. It is vain to repeat that the GCD is not "legislation" and hence can be twisted any way the new religious education wishes. The Holy See is not accustomed to issuing documents so that they can be distorted and undermined; it issues "directories" so that they may direct. *Focus,* meanwhile, is determined to press on with its own brand of catechesis in spite of the plain language of the GCD, asserting on page 18 that "catechetical programs which are blind to the inevitability of on-going change in society in general and the Church in particular can only tragically retard the religious development of students who must live in the world of tomorrow". "Process" and "change" are the keys here, then, not the content of the faith: "Jesus Christ . . . the same yesterday, today, and forever" (Heb 13:8).

Much more could be said about this singular commentary on the *General Catechetical Directory,* as it is called. For example, the notes (pp. 100–101) reveal that nearly every scholarly reference contained in *Focus* is to an overt public dissenter from Catholic teaching. Thus, the expert quoted to establish that sin is something different from what the GCD's "law-orientation" provides for is none other than Father Charles E. Curran, professor at the Catholic University of America until he was let go as a result of the decision of the Congregation for the Doctrine of the Faith that he was no longer a Catholic theologian. Similarly, dissenter Gregory Baum is the primary authority cited by *Focus* on the subject of revelation, dissenter John Dedek is cited in favor of the fundamental option theory (contrary to Rome's *Persona Humana,* no. 10), and dissenter Richard P. McBrien is quoted to prove that the Church and the Kingdom are not the same (contrary to *Lumen Gentium,* no. 3).

If the *General Catechetical Directory* was prepared and published, at least in part, in order to put an end to what the GCD in its foreword called "the errors which are not infrequently noted in catechetics today", then *Focus on American Catechetics* can be said to have very effectively neutralized the GCD's expected effect by substituting its own views on crucial topics. With such immediate access to the religious education establishment, it would not be surprising to find more religion teachers referring to and being guided by *Focus* than referring to and being guided by the GCD itself. This may not have been the first time that a Roman document intended to clear up some of the confusion in the Church was instead undermined by some of the very people whose responsibility it was to implement it; but this was a particularly serious case of it.

5.

The National Conference of Diocesan Directors of Religious Education may well have been successful in neutralizing the effect of Rome's *General Catechetical Directory* by producing a commentary on it more to their own liking. However, they were unable to stop the chronic complaints about the perceived deficiencies of Catholic religious education. These complaints went on, and, as the NCEA's own Religious Education Outcomes Inventory was later to show, there was a very real basis for them; the kids did *not* know their faith.

Focus on American Catechetics had reassured its clientele (p. 64) that, "while there may remain some confusion in regard to the GCD's position on the use of formulas, it is evident that the document does not intend that educators return to the discredited methodology of yesteryear". On the evidence, it surely would appear to have been the new catechesis that featured a "discredited methodology", quite inadequate to the task of imparting the faith. However, the religious education establishment did not appear to be bothered by this, by and large, and so the new catechesis went grinding on regardless.

Conscious of continuing difficulties and confusion in religious education, the National Conference of Catholic Bishops (NCCB) decided to issue a document of its own on the subject in order to try to clear up some of the confusion. This was the genesis for the U.S. bishops' *Basic Teachings for Catholic Religious Education,* issued in January 1973.[26] This was a very concise document containing

[26] National Conference of Catholic Bishops, *Basic Teachings for Catholic Religious Education* (Washington, D.C.: Publications Office, United States Catholic Conference, January 11, 1973).

only what the bishops called "the principal elements of the Christian message". "It is necessary", the bishops specified in their introduction, "that these basic teachings be central in all Catholic religious instruction, be never overlooked or minimized, and be given adequate and frequent emphasis."[27] It was really quite exceptional that the American bishops should have thought it necessary to issue these *Basic Teachings,* especially since the GCD's chapter 2 already summed up, concisely but adequately, "the more outstanding elements of the Christian message"; and also because the bishops had already decided at their semiannual meeting in April 1972 to sponsor an extensive national consultation process looking toward the preparation and publication of a *National Catechetical Directory* (NCD) for Catholics of the United States. The *General Catechetical Directory* had provided and had perhaps assumed that national directories would be prepared for each country or region.[28] The development of this NCD for the United States will be covered in a subsequent section of this chapter. Why *Basic Teachings,* which would almost necessarily be an interim document, also had to be issued was never fully explained. The bishops were quite circumspect about their real intentions, but one strong clue about why they found the statement necessary is found in the introduction to the *Basic Teachings:* "It is necessary", the bishops specified, "that the authentic teachings of the Church, and those only, be presented in religious instruction as official Catholic doctrine. Religion texts or classroom teachers should never present merely subjective theorizing as the Church's teaching." This statement could well have been prompted by the continuing, indeed incessant, complaints of pastors, parents, and teachers about the glaring doctrinal deficiencies of the current catechesis.

But perhaps the bishops should have included a further statement to the effect that classroom teachers should spend less time "helping the student reflect on his own experience" and trying to

[27] Ibid., p. 1.

[28] Sacred Congregation for the Clergy, *General Catechetical Directory* (Washington, D.C.: United States Catholic Conference Publications Office, 1971), Foreword, nos. 88 and 134.

provide "real and vicarious experiences", in the words of *Focus on American Catechetics.* For the problem of defective religious education was only in part a problem of errors, distortions, and omissions in doctrine; another part of the problem was the preoccupation of religion teachers with psychological factors that had little to do with teaching anything at all. But by 1973 it is not clear that the bishops had really taken in the implications of the decisive shifts that had occurred in the catechetical movement, if indeed they have taken them in to this day. The process of consultations for the American NCD was similarly to show that neither the bishops, nor Catholics generally, really understood very well where the professional religious educators were coming from. Even though the NCD was to end up as a useful and orthodox document, in part through the decisive intervention of many bishops, as will be recounted later, this result came about because in the end the bishops instinctively took a stand affirming the faith of the Church of which they are the official teachers. Naturally they should have taken their stand on the faith of the Church; but they did so in this instance without really understanding what the religious educators were up to and what it was they were obliged to counter.

For example, just two months before the American bishops issued the *Basic Teachings for Catholic Religious Education,* they issued another major statement about Catholic education in general. This was their Pastoral Message *To Teach as Jesus Did.*[29] It was basically a very positive message, recommitting the Church to the message of Christ (*didache*), to fellowship and community in the Holy Spirit (*Koinonia*), and to service to the Christian and human communities (*diakonia*). Among other things, this Pastoral Message gave welcome encouragement to Catholic schools at a very difficult time for these institutions. Although *To Teach as Jesus Did* was not intended to be a substitute either for the forthcoming *Basic Teachings* or for the *National Catechetical Directory* to be

[29] National Conference of Catholic Bishops, *To Teach as Jesus Did: A Pastoral Message on Catholic Education,* November, 1972.

prepared later, it did touch upon catechesis and included the following comment:

> Although religious education should foster unity within the family and the Church, today at times it causes division instead. There are several reasons for this. Changes in religious education in recent years have disturbed many parents, in part at least because the training their children now receive seems to bear little resemblance to their own. To the extent that this problem relates to valid pedagogical methods, it may be resolved as parents come to understand better the techniques of contemporary religious education. However, the difficulty also touches at times on more basic issues involving the orthodoxy and authenticity of what is taught.[30]

It will be noted that the bishops themselves employ here the rationalization so often used to put down protesting parents, namely, that the deficiencies perceived by parents in the religious education of their children really amount only to "differences" from the way the parents themselves were taught. Obviously there was more to it than that; nor was it merely a matter of teaching techniques or pedagogy, as the bishops themselves conceded in mentioning "orthodoxy" and "authenticity"—though it is remarkable how delicately they do touch upon these subjects. Nevertheless it is also clear that they recognized a problem, although it was not so clear to them what they could or should have been doing about it. That this should have been the case more than a decade after the catechetical movement had shifted over to anthropocentric and psychological catechesis indicated how much they still had to learn which their experts had not told them.

Still, the issuance of *Basic Teachings for Catholic Religious Education* only two months after the above-quoted paragraph saw the light of day was a very firm and positive goodwill effort on the part of the American bishops to try to remedy what ailed Catholic religious education. How did the *Basic Teachings* fare? In particular, how were they received by the religious education

[30] Ibid., no. 53.

establishment? Did the NCDDRE perhaps decide to do another commentary on *them?* No: this time it was the Division of Religious Education-CCD of the bishops' own United States Catholic Conference (USCC) that produced the document intended to undermine what the bishops themselves had stipulated in the *Basic Teachings,* just as *Focus on American Catechetics* had undermined the *General Catechetical Directory.*

In the fall of 1974, the Division of Religious Education-CCD of the USCC published a booklet similar in size and format to the *Basic Teachings* and clearly intended to be a companion booklet to the latter. Its title was: *A Study Aid for Basic Teachings for Catholic Religious Education.*[31] It consisted almost entirely of a list of books recommended by this USCC religious education office for all those who were teaching religion in Catholic schools and CCD programs.

It was surprising, to put it mildly, that any such thing as a *Study Aid* should have been thought necessary for a document as simple, fundamental, and irreducible as, by definition, the *Basic Teachings* were. It was as surprising as that, earlier, a commentary on the *General Catechetical Directory* had been thought necessary. Nevertheless, the *Study Aid* was produced; it listed eighty-two different books that were recommended to religion teachers. Teachers were supposed to read and consult these books in order to assist them in their task of catechesis.

It would obviously be beyond the scope of this study to provide an evaluation of all of the eighty-two books recommended to religion teachers by the *Study Aid.* In order to realize how radically and thoroughly the USCC *Study Aid* really served to undermine the U.S. bishops' own *Basic Teachings,* however, it will be necessary to provide a sufficient number of sample quotations of the kinds of things being recommended to the teachers who were supposed to be following and implementing the *Basic Teachings.*

[31] Division of Religious Education-CCD, United States Catholic Conference, *A Study Aid for Basic Teachings for Catholic Religious Education* (Washington, D.C.: 1974).

In what follows, a quotation from the *Basic Teachings* setting forth one of the doctrines that the bishops specified must "be central in all Catholic religious instruction [and] never be overlooked or minimized" will be given; and following that, a sample quotation or two on the same subject from one or more of the books recommended by the *Study Aid* will be provided by contrast. The reader may then judge whether the recommended books appear to support, or to undermine, the doctrines the bishops were insisting upon. What should be clear is that any religion teacher turning to at least some of the books recommended would encounter doctrines entirely at variance with what he was supposed to be teaching in the classroom by the specific mandate of the American bishops. So the dilemma is created: should the religion teacher follow the plain words of the shepherds of the Church or succumb to the blandishments of the new theology with its new and variant interpretations of various doctrines of the faith?

Obviously the following quotations are merely samples. Anyone prepared to go over the entire list of eighty-two recommended books would have quite a task to carry out; but the samples included here are certainly not unrepresentative of the kinds of things recommended by the *Study Aid* generally; the following citations are not taken out of context but represent what the recommended books generally advance, as opposed to what the Church teaches. But what clearly emerges out of all this is another case where an official Church bureau was found to be working at cross purposes with the bishops, while actually working under the auspices of the bishops.

1. *Basic Teachings:* "In the Old Testament God revealed himself as the one true personal God, transcendent above this world." *Study Aid* recommended book: "The manner of thinking and speaking about God in traditional Christian piety, and even in most professional theology, is no longer in harmony with the contemporary experience of reality. What is wrong, for today, in the traditional manner is the objectification of God. Because of the change in the understanding of man and his world, it has become impossible to think of God as a being over and above

human history" (from Gregory Baum, *New Horizon: Theological Essays* [Mahwah, N.J.: Paulist Press, 1972], pp. 56–57).

2. *Basic Teachings:* "As the Messiah fulfilling Old Testament prophecy and history, Jesus . . . preached the Gospel of the Kingdom of God and summoned men to interior conversion and faith." *Study Aid* recommended book: "Christ does not supply any ready-made answers for the questions of contemporary men. His life is not proposed as an answer to the questions which man's being presupposes. He gives no revealed doctrines about God nor any revealed precepts for leading a proper life" (Gabriel Moran, in Daniel Callahan, ed., *God, Jesus, Spirit* [New York: Herder and Herder, 1969], p. 13).

3. *Basic Teachings:* "Christ directed his apostles to teach the observance of everything that he had commanded." *Study Aid* recommended book: ". . . Christian faith is not the acceptance of a body of doctrines nor is it the observance of laws or the performance of cult . . . " (Bernard J. Cooke, *The God of Space and Time* [New York: Holt, Rinehart, and Winston, 1969], p. 141).

4. *Basic Teachings:* " . . . It is the duty of the teaching authority, or magisterium, to give guidance for applying the enduring norms and values of Christian morality to specific situations of everyday life." *Study Aid* recommended book: "Seeking moral guidance through our Roman Catholic Church alone is an appeal which we are not wise to make in any Christian matter, doctrinal or moral" (Rev. Gerard S. Sloyan, *How Do I Know I'm Doing Right?* [Dayton, Ohio: Pflaum, 1966], p. 116).

5. *Basic Teachings* (quoting Vatican II's *Gaudium et Spes,* no. 13): "Although he was made by God in a state of holiness, from the very dawn of history man abused his liberty, at the urging of the Evil One. Man set himself against God and sought to find fulfillment apart from God." *Study Aid* recommended book: "The difficulties surrounding this presentation of original sin are so many and at times so intractable that they certainly demand the radical rethinking of the doctrine that is going on in contemporary theology" (James P. Mackey, in Michael J. Taylor, ed., *The*

Mystery of Sin and Forgiveness [New York: Alba House, 1970], p. 218).

6. *Basic Teachings* (quoting Rom 5:12): "Through one man sin entered the world, and with sin death, death thus coming to all men inasmuch as all sinned." *Study Aid* recommended book: "The traditional explanation pointed to a single sin of the first parent; ours contends that the fall is the whole history of sinful deeds. . . . The notion that the whole human race has descended from one couple seems a presupposition based on an outdated picture of the world" (Piet Schoonenberg, S.J., in Michael J. Taylor, ed., *The Mystery of Sin and Forgiveness* [New York: Alba House, 1970], pp. 249–50).

7. *Basic Teachings:* "The creation of angels and of the world is the beginning of the mystery of salvation." *Study Aid* recommended book: "The very existence of the devil and his attendant demons, and thus the existence of a class of damned persons other than human beings, has now become open to question" (Robert Nowell, *What a Modern Catholic Believes about Death* [Chicago: Thomas More Press, 1972], p. 93).

6.

When the *General Catechetical Directory* came out in 1971, it envisaged the preparation and publication of national or regional catechetical directories.[32] At their spring meeting in April 1972, the bishops of the United States voted to go ahead with the preparation of a *National Catechetical Directory* for Catholics of the United States. A special committee for the project was named, headed by Archbishop John F. Whealon of Hartford (who had also chaired the bishops' committee charged with producing the *Basic Teachings*). The committee for the NCD had three other bishops on it plus "eight other members who were a microcosm of the Church in this country—a black, a chicano, parents, priests,

[32] Sacred Congregation for Clergy, *General Catechetical Directory,* Foreword, nos. 88 and 134.

nuns, and a brother".[33] A priest of the Diocese of Manchester, New Hampshire, Monsignor Wilfrid H. Paradis, was named project director, and Sister Mariella Frye, a Mission Helper of the Sacred Heart, was named associate project director.

According to one account, concrete plans for an American NCD actually originated in discussions among some of the leading lights and gurus of the American catechetical movement at a religious education conference held in Miami in October 1971 (following the International Catechetical Congress held in Rome earlier, at which the GCD had been effectively unveiled). The religious educators meeting in Miami were said to have observed that "the process could be as important as the product".[34] This phrase is not a bad description of how the catechetical movement had come to regard catechesis generally. If the religious education establishment expected to control the "process" of producing an American directory, though, they were going to be disappointed in the end, as it turned out. In the event, the nationwide NCD consultation process proved to be of such interest and importance to the bishops, the Catholic laity, and those religious educators still interested in imparting the faith of Christ rather than trying to create interesting experiences in the classroom, that the NCD ended up being so sound a basic document that even Rome had few corrections to make (although it did have some). This was not, however, because the religious education establishment did not try to keep the NCD consultation process in its own hands; it simply did not succeed in doing so.

From these unlikely beginnings, though, many years would elapse before a text of the NCD could be approved by the bishops; this was to be in November 1977. It was nearly a year later, in October 1978, before this text was approved for publication by the Congregation for the Clergy in Rome, with stipulations for several changes added. The final approved and definitive

[33] Berard L. Marthaler, Ph.D., "*Sharing the Light of Faith:* New Guidelines for Roman Catholic Catechesis", in *Military Chaplain's Review,* Fall 1978.

[34] Mary Charles Bryce, "*Sharing the Light of Faith:* Catechetical Threshold for the U.S. Church", in Warren, ed., *Sourcebook,* p. 263.

text of the NCD was published in 1979 under the title *Sharing the Light of Faith,* after eight years of massive consultations and efforts, drafts and redrafts.[35]

The bishops had all along envisaged extensive national consultations. The first such consultation took place between December 1973 and March 1974. A fifty-eight-page booklet with the title "Towards a National Catechetical Directory" was quite widely circulated for comments and suggestions. Many individual meetings were held (over four thousand) and over seventeen hundred responses were received from 113 dioceses (83 percent of all dioceses).[36] Most of those who took part in this first consultation remember the first draft as quite bad—almost a caricature or parody of the doctrineless, experiential type of catechesis that had unfortunately become so widespread. Strong reactions to the draft, demanding recognizable Catholic faith and doctrine, especially by the laity, gave considerable pause to any who had conceived the consultations as a process designed to baptize the new catechesis; the new catechesis proved to have aroused scepticism and resistance wherever people had a chance to express their views about it.

The second consultation, which took place in January–April 1975, was much larger, and great credit has to be given to the directory committee for making it possible. Over 650,000 copies of the draft text were circulated, plus another 6,000 copies of a Spanish translation. A simply massive response ensued; over seventy-six thousand recommendations or suggestions for changes or improvements were received.[37] Again, the recommendations coming from the laity and lay groups included many clear, strong, and insistent voices for doctrine and orthodoxy. One of the benefits of

[35] National Conference of Catholic Bishops (NCCB), *Sharing the Light of Faith: National Catechetical Directory for Catholics of the United States* (Washington, D.C.: 1979). Text approved by the NCCB at their general meeting, November 14–17, 1977; approved by the Sacred Congregation for the Clergy, Second Office, October 30, 1978.

[36] Bryce, "Catechetical Threshold for Church", p. 263.

[37] Marthaler, "New Guidelines for Catechesis".

the consultation process was that voices were allowed to be heard that too often are not heard on topics in which entrenched bureaucracies have vested interests.

On the basis of this mass consultation, a revised text was prepared and was ready at the beginning of 1977. This time around, mass consultations were eschewed. Instead the third consultation took place in the individual dioceses, and 86 percent of all U.S. dioceses participated in this third and final round. The NCD committee was definitely hearing the voice of the faithful in more ways than one. For example, it had been decided with this draft that the *Basic Teachings* would be incorporated into the NCD *in toto.* Father Berard Marthaler later candidly explained:

> After several alternatives were discussed, the Directory committee decided to incorporate the substance of the entire text of the *Basic Teachings.* The document had won wide acceptance among conservatives who were concerned about the "content" of Catholic religious education which to them meant *doctrine. Basic Teachings* purports to be inspired by the principles of Vatican II and the *General Catechetical Directory,* but it has an unmistakable Tridentine accent which betrays its parentage. By incorporating the text of the *Basic Teachings* in the revised draft circulated in the second consultation, the committee opened the door for some modifications of the text. The principal changes are found in articles dealing with morality. They were amended to include points from two other documents which were promulgated after the *Basic Teachings* had appeared: *To Live in Christ Jesus,* a pastoral reflection on the moral life issued by the American bishops in 1976; and the *Declaration on Certain Questions Concerning Sexual Ethics* [*Persona Humana*] issued by the Roman Congregation for Doctrine in December, 1975.[38]

Those critical of the new catechesis as manifested in successive drafts of the NCD hardly objected to the use of these two documents from the American bishops and the Congregation for the Doctrine of the Faith, respectively; the latter of the two docu-

[38] Ibid.

ments has in fact been referred to more than once in the course of the present study. What was most significant here, though, was that the inclusion of the *Basic Teachings* in the NCD *meant* that henceforth the document could not endorse the new catechesis in unalloyed form; it meant that the NCD was going to be a real Catholic document, requiring doctrinal content, in the end.

The text that went to the individual dioceses for the third consultation at the beginning of 1977 was still far from perfect. A very widely circulated pamphlet published by the national lay association, Catholics United for the Faith, around this same time detailed many of the deficiencies remaining in what was nevertheless recognized to be a much improved draft; by its title this pamphlet indicated one of the chief deficiencies that still remained: *"Man Shall Not Live by 'Experience' Alone"*.[39]

For the old controversy over revelation and experience still raged; it was essential to the new catechesis to have some version of its concept of on-going revelation adopted; otherwise, what *was* the point of experiential catechesis? What the text finally ended up presenting to the bishops (which actually survived until corrected by Rome) was the following:

> The word "revelation" is used throughout this Directory to refer both to that public Revelation which closed at the end of the Apostolic Age and to other forms of revelation through which God manifests and communicates Himself through His presence in the Church and the world. Whenever the word is used to refer to public Revelation, it is capitalized. Whenever it refers to other than public revelation, it is not capitalized: and, when used with this meaning in the form of a verb, it is written within single quotes.[40]

It is hard to imagine a more labored and contrived compromise used to paper over two views of revelation that were in reality

[39] *"Man Shall Not Live by 'Experience' Alone": An Analysis of the Draft National Catechetical Directory* (New Rochelle, N.Y.: Catholics United for the Faith, January, 1977).

[40] Quoted by Marthaler, "New Guidelines for Catechesis".

simply incompatible. It is even harder to imagine why such a compromise was thought to be necessary considering that the *General Catechetical Directory* (no. 13) had already made the proper distinction, and quite clearly: "The divine revelation which constitutes the object of the Catholic faith and which was completed at the time of the apostles, must be clearly distinguished from the grace of the Holy Spirit, without whose inspiration and illumination no one can believe." Nevertheless it has to be conceded that the religious educators no doubt felt very strongly about their exaggerated view of on-going revelation, and they were evidently not going to give it up unless compelled to do so. To jump ahead on this same subject for a moment, it is interesting to see how this same paragraph reads in the final, approved version of the NCD, after correction by Rome:

> The word "revelation" is used in this document to refer to that divine public revelation which closed at the end of the Apostolic Age. The terms "manifestation" and "communication" are used for the other modes by which God continues to make Himself known and share Himself with human beings through his presence in the Church and the world.[41]

All is surely well that ends well. Before the NCD got to the point where the Congregation was able to put these final finishing touches on it, however, it also had to pass muster with the American bishops. The final draft prepared by the NCD committee following the third consultation was submitted to the bishops for consideration at their fall meeting, November 14–17, 1977.

Some 350 amendments to the final draft were submitted by the bishops and were voted upon in the course of the meeting. The amendment process proved, in several respects, to be essential. Up until that time, there was a growing feeling that with each succeeding draft's attempt to be acceptable to the various and even opposing positions of those commenting on the text, the overall effectiveness and credibility of the final version was being seri-

[41] NCCB, *National Catechetical Directory,* no. 50, p. 28.

ously compromised. One wag hailed the genius of the draft text "which can, within one and the same paragraph, encompass not only both extremes but numbers of middles, delivering itself of the whole with such ineffable finesse that all parties can think themselves unambiguously either sustained or stranded in their views".[42]

More than one hundred amendments were approved by way of adding, deleting, or amending paragraphs and sections of the *Directory*. Although some of these revisions were principally stylistic, a number of them altered the NCD significantly and for the better in several key sections. On November 17, 1977, the bishops, by a vote of 216 in favor to 12 opposed, directed that the document be submitted to Rome for final approval. Some religious educators, reacting to the amendment process effected by the bishops, expressed the view that the bishops had "almost ravaged the document" or had "turned it around 140 degrees".[43]

One of the most significant of all the episcopal amendments offered and accepted was introduced by the late Cardinal Terence Cooke, archbishop of New York; this amendment concerned the always hotly debated topic of "memorization"; Cardinal Cooke's amendment resulted in the following significant paragraph being included in the document as it reads in the final, approved version; by itself, its inclusion included a signal victory over watered-down, doctrineless catechesis:

> In every age and culture Christianity has commended certain prayers, formulas, and practices to all members of the faith community, even the youngest. While catechesis cannot be limited to the repetition of formulas and it is essential that formulas and facts pertaining to faith be understood, memorization has nevertheless had a special place in the handing-on of the faith throughout the ages and should continue to have a

[42] Didier-Jacques Piveteau and James T. Dillon, *Resurgence of Religious Education* (Notre Dame, Ind.: Religious Education Press, 1977), p. 214.

[43] Quoted by Michael J. Wrenn, "Religious Education at the Crossroads: U.S.A.", in Dermot A. Lane, ed., *Religious Education and the Future* (Dublin, Ireland: Columba Press, 1986), p. 42.

place today, especially in catechetical programs for the young. It should be adapted to the level and ability of the child and introduced in a gradual manner, through a process which, begun early, continues gradually, flexibly, and never slavishly. In this way certain elements of Catholic faith, tradition, and practice are learned for a lifetime and can contribute to the individual's continued growth in understanding and living the faith.[44]

Nearly a year elapsed following the submission to Rome of the version approved by the U.S. bishops of what had come to be titled *Sharing the Light of Faith: National Catechetical Directory for Catholics of the United States.* Then, in a letter dated October 30, 1978, and addressed to Archbishop John Quinn, then president of the National Conference of Catholic Bishops, the Congregation for the Clergy commended *Sharing the Light of Faith* for:

> ... being a generally faithful application of the *General Catechetical Directory* to the American scene. It is outstanding for its ecclesial spirit, its clarity of expression, its emphasis on memorization of basic prayers and doctrinal formulations, its solid argument, its flexibility. The substantial orthodoxy of *Sharing the Light of Faith* should be apparent to anyone who studies the entire work attentively. Doctrinal statements that may seem incomplete at first reading of one section are habitually rounded out in another.

Having delivered itself of these initial encomiums, the letter went on to indicate that "there are certain points of importance that should be re-worked before the publication of the first edition."

Regarding the compromise position that the authors of the NCD had taken on the question of revelation, employing a capital "R" to refer to that public revelation that closed at the end of the apostolic age, as opposed to the use of a lower case "r" for those manifestations of God other than the public revelation, the letter from the Congregation observed:

[44] NCCB, *National Catechetical Directory,* no. 176(e), p. 102.

> The employment of capital and small letters (Revelation, revelation) to distinguish various meanings of the notion of revelation tends to engender confusion. It would seem to be less open to misunderstanding, if the word "revelation" standing alone, without modifiers, quotation marks or italics, were to signify public, divine revelation in the strict sense, and that other expressions be chosen to indicate other modes by which God manifests Himself to men.

Likewise, on the position adopted by the NCD committee regarding the question of preparation for and reception of the sacraments of penance and first Eucharist, the letter observed: "Not only should the catechesis for the Sacrament of Reconciliation precede First Holy Communion, but youngsters should normally *receive* the Sacrament of Penance before their First Communion."

The section of the NCD that dealt with the administration of General Absolution was said to require the reflection of existing norms by indicating more clearly that General Absolution is not only rarely to be extended but also that the circumstances determining its administration should be serious. The specific nature of the priesthood was shown to need a more exact expression by placing appropriate emphasis on both its sacrificial-eucharistic aspect and on the concept of the configuration of the priest to Christ. The ministerial priest acts not only in the name of Christ but "in the person of Christ". Also, the character of the priest and bishop was cited as needing to be more clearly distinguished from that of the deacon as well as from the common priesthood of the faithful, which differs from the ministerial or hierarchical priesthood "essentially and not only in degree".[45]These changes were made.

Thus, after a prolonged process of nearly eight years, Catholics of the United States ended up with a *National Catechetical Directory* not only worthy of the name but corrective at many crucial junctures of many of the mistakes made in catechesis in the postconciliar era. In addition to the salutary correctives inherent

[45] The October 30, 1978, letter from the Congregation for the Clergy quoted in Wrenn, "Religious Education at Crossroads", 1988, pp. 42–43.

in the NCD's treatment of revelation and memorization, already noted, *Sharing the Light of Faith* also went on record as saying such things as the following (which are merely highlights of the document, selected practically at random):

—"Critical scholarship of itself is not the ultimate source of the full interpretation of the sacred texts" (no. 60).

—"Catechists teach as authentic doctrines only those truths which the magisterium teaches" (no. 60).

—*Lumen Gentium,* no. 25, on the necessity for "religious assent", even in the course of ordinary teaching, is endorsed; hence "dissent" from ordinary teachings is necessarily excluded (no. 93).

—The Credo of the People of God of Pope Paul VI is quoted as an authority on the doctrine of original sin (no. 92) and is otherwise represented as an authentic expression of the Church's magisterium.

—"In view of the present tragic reality of legalized abortion practiced on a massive scale in our country, followers of Christ are obliged not only to be personally opposed to abortion, but to seek to remove circumstances which influence some to turn to abortion as a solution to their problems and also work for the restoration of a climate of opinion and a legal order which respect the value of unborn human life" (no. 105; this, by the way, eliminates the excuse of those Catholic politicians who declare that they are personally opposed to abortion but . . .).

—The Sacrament of Reconciliation normally should be celebrated prior to the reception of First Communion" (no. 126).

—"Mortal sin is found 'in every deliberate transgression in serious matter, of each of the moral laws, and not only in formal and direct resistance to the commandment of charity' " (chap. 5, no. 33; this, of course, is an explicit rejection of the so-called fundamental option theory).

—"It is the task of catechesis to elicit *assent* to all that the Church teaches (no. 190; emphasis added).

In short, *Sharing the Light of Faith* turned out to be a guide to catechesis that, if followed, would have served to attenuate or eliminate many of the deficiencies that had become chronic. How it was received by the religious education establishment is a subject that will have to be looked at next. It certainly should have been seriously consulted and followed by the Woodstock group of Catholic scholars before they ever launched out on their pretentious effort to tell American Catholics what the shape of their religious education should be in *The Universal Catechism Reader.*

7.

Sharing the Light of Faith was the first *national catechetical directory* to be submitted by a national hierarchy to the Holy See for approval. It is evident from the letter from the Congregation for the Clergy approving it that there was deep satisfaction with the final product, the fruit of the most extensive consultation in the history of the Catholic Church in this country.

Here was a catechetical tool that did more than express a keen awareness of the contemporary Catholic scene in the United States. Whether the issue was that of content versus experience, the inductive method of catechesis versus the deductive, religious education as a cognitive versus an affective enterprise, the Christian community versus the institutional model of the Church, or so on, the NCD exhibited a very balanced approach. It did this by showing how each of the aforementioned elements could be blended to achieve a catechesis that would consistently be both authentic in doctrine and moral practice as well as contemporary in its recourse to tried and proven methodologies.

Unfortunately once again, the ink was barely dry on the pages of this attractively printed document before many of the solid principles and positions set forth in its pages began to be explained away by some of the very people most directly responsible for implementing the NCD. Catechetical revisionism began again in earnest.

One who has read the present study up to this point might well be pardoned for asking pointedly whether it was the National

Conference of Diocesan Directors of Religious Education, or some department or division of the United States Catholic Conference, that moved in to undermine what was supposed to have been an American Catholic consensus on the subject of religious education—a consensus achieved only at the cost of much time, toil, and true compromise on all sides. It will be recalled, of course, as recounted above, that it was the NCDDRE and the USCC Division of Religious Education-CCD, respectively, that moved against Rome's *General Catechetical Directory* and the U.S. bishops' *Basic Teachings for Catholic Religious Education.* Actually, *both* the NCDDRE and the USCC moved against the NCD in their various ways, as will now be recounted.

In April 1979, the NCDDRE published what it called a *Discussion Guide to Sharing the Light of Faith.*[46] The *Discussion Guide* was authored by the same Father Thomas Sullivan responsible for the earlier *Focus on American Catechetics,* reviewed above, and utilizes some of the same techniques as the earlier work. There is a brief summary of the contents of the NCD, followed by questions about it and recommended readings for the religion teacher (which, if actually read, like the books recommended in the USCC *Study Aid for Basic Teachings for Catholic Religious Education,* would only serve to undermine what the official Church document says, since many of the books recommended are by open dissenters from Catholic teaching).

Reading the *Discussion Guide for Sharing the Light of Faith,* and especially the manner in which the questions are phrased, soon makes it apparent that this *Discussion Guide* is really another advocacy text justifying the continued retention in catechesis of a number of viewpoints considered to have been corrected in the final published version of *Sharing the Light of Faith* itself; questions thought to have been settled by the consultation process for producing the NCD are raised all over again and put back up for

[46] Rev. Thomas F. Sullivan, *Discussion Guide to Sharing the Light of Faith* (Washington, D.C.: National Conference of Diocesan Directors of Religious Education, 1979).

grabs as if they had not already been considered and ultimately rejected in the course of the Church's official wide-ranging deliberations. Space does not allow for a detailed analysis of the various questions and the beneath-the-surface agendas that they represent; but the fact is that the *Discussion Guide* again became a vehicle for disseminating on the local diocesan or parochial level viewpoints that did not always square either with the teachings of the Church in general or the directives of the NCD in particular.

Space allows only for a couple of representative examples of how the *Discussion Guide* consistently proceeds. For example, commenting on the section of the NCD where it is made quite clear, as already brought out above, that revelation properly speaking ended in the apostolic age, the *Discussion Guide* then asks, disingenuously: " 'There can be no new public revelation.... Yet God continues to manifest Himself.' What are some of the ways God has *revealed* himself to you?" (emphasis added).[47] In other words, the question deliberately eliminates the very distinction intended by the NCD, as stipulated by Rome in this case; it does this by first covering over part of the explanation given in the NCD with ellipses; then, in the very next sentence, it goes right back to equating "manifesting" with "revealing" again, as if the Holy See had never insisted upon the distinction that it did, in fact, insist upon.

Or again, the *Discussion Guide* asks: "Must we still believe in original sin?"[48] This happens to be a doctrine of the Church that was irrevocably defined by the Council of Trent, as the NCD specifies; yet directors of religious education nevertheless feel themselves wholly entitled to ask whether Catholics must "still" believe in it, the suggestion being that there might indeed be doctrines once defined that Catholics no longer have to believe in. On the same page the *Discussion Guide* goes on to ask if Catholics "must *blindly* follow the teaching of the Church" (emphasis added), as if that were the customary manner Catholics receive teachings

[47] Ibid., p. 12.
[48] Ibid., p. 23.

guaranteed by the Holy Spirit; this way of treating the subject matter represents a deliberate disparagement of the tenets of the Catholic faith as traditionally received and held by Catholics. It is remarkable that such a disparagement of the faith can occur in respect to the NCD, whose *raison d'etre* is supposed to be the imparting of that same faith.

Finally, although the NCD itself clearly establishes that First Confession must precede First Communion, as brought out above, the *Discussion Guide* nevertheless feels able to ask, blandly: "Why do many authorities recommend a later age?"[49]

These examples must suffice; the pattern of what is being done is very clear, whether in this document, or earlier ones reviewed produced by the religious education establishment. The technique employed is very insidious, of course, but probably all too effective: the religious education establishment never gave up when it came to calling into question and dissenting from things that, over and over again, the Church had tried to settle. The fact that the *Discussion Guide* was really subversive of *Sharing the Light of Faith* rather than constituting a legitimate commentary upon it did not, of course, prevent this vintage NCDDRE production from being widely distributed by the Department of Education of the United States Catholic Conference; no conflict was apparently perceived in this agency of the U.S. bishops engaged in bringing discredit upon a document solemnly approved and promulgated by those same bishops after approval by the Holy See.

This bureau of the USCC went even farther. It sponsored a special issue on the NCD in the professional religious education journal it publishes, *The Living Light.*[50] Just as the *Discussion Guide* sought to raise once again and legitimate a number of questions considered settled as a result of the NCD national consultation process, the amendments made at the fall 1977 bishops' meeting, and the October 1978 letter from the Congregation for the Clergy, so this special issue vigorously attempted to explain

[49] Ibid., p. 29.
[50] *The Living Light,* Summer 1979.

away a number of the substantive areas on which the final published version of the NCD had been both clear and unambiguous. The technique employed on this occasion was the scholarly journal article authored by acknowledged religious education "experts" (some of whom are still active in training religion teachers to this day).

Writing in the foreword, the same ubiquitous Reverend Thomas Sullivan introduced the articles to follow by observing, among other things, that "the Church in our day is not, however, of one mind in all things, and the *Directory* understandably reflects some of the ambiguity of the current scene".[51] It is not unfair to describe Father Sullivan's position here as follows: the Church decides her policy and program for religious education in *Sharing the Light of Faith* and promulgates it to the whole Church in the United States, after allowing virtually everyone to get his point of view on record beforehand, but the religious educators still disagree; *therefore* "the Church in our day is not . . . of one mind".

In her article, Sister Anne Marie Mongoven, O.P., still apparently going strong today at catechetical summer institutes and the like, observed that "the *Directory* reflects our diversity and unity. Every reader can look at and find whatever he or she wants to see. It is both liberal and conservative in what it says, because we are both liberal and conservative."[52] Such political terms, of course, do not, and cannot, apply to the faith; where the faith itself is concerned, Catholics should not be—and the NCD is not—either liberal or conservative; but Sister Mongoven's position certainly makes it easy to interpret the NCD entirely in accordance with one's tastes.

In his article "Revelation: Dimensions and Issues", William P. Loewe, Ph.D., of the Catholic University of America presented a study of the notion of continuing revelation as it emerged in the religious education enterprise in recent years and found its way into successive drafts of the NCD. This author actually quoted the

[51] Ibid., "Editor's Foreword", p. 133.
[52] Ibid., p. 136.

letter from the Congregation for the Clergy correcting the compromise position of employing a capital "R" and a lower case "r"—the NCD committee pleaded with the bishops to retain this feature in spite of Rome's judgment! In spite of the fact that the Roman correction was accepted, Loewe was able to employ his own hermeneutic to reassure the readers of *The Living Light* that all had not been lost in reconciling the poles of tension between the notion of continuing revelation and the affirmation of a public revelation completed with the death of the last apostle. Thus he observed: "The final version of Chapter Three contains the substance, if not the language of continuing revelation. A compromise document, it reproduces the tensions inherent in the theological pluralism which characterizes the Church today."[53] Here, then, *is* an example of interpreting the NCD entirely in accordance with one's tastes.

Reverend Michael D. Place, S.T.D., formerly of Saint Mary of the Lake Seminary in Mundelein, Illinois, in his article "Reflections of a Moral Theologian", examined the methodology or framework in which ethical reflection takes place. He contrasted the historicist perspective of the concrete, the individual, and the changing with what he called the older approach in ethics and theology in general that began with the abstract, the ethical, the essential, and the unchanging. Change is to be taken seriously, he thought, and "obviously change in areas such as family life or sexuality or the state would have significant import for ethical thought and would suggest the possibility of modification of earlier ethical conclusions". He then considered the context in which ethical reflection takes place, especially in the light of "the reforming works of Fuchs and Häring", and the "image of the human person" recently proposed in the latter's new work, *Free and Faithful in Christ.* In speaking of the many conflict situations that people face in seeking to be responsible and relational, the author went on:

> They are faced with the question of how they are to make decisions about the appropriateness of specific actions when

[53] Ibid., p. 167.

some conflict arises. In the older tradition such conflict was recognized and addressed by the ethical principle of double effect. While still of value, that principle is today found by many moralists to be too limited in its application. Thus, they have developed what is known as the principle of proportionality as a guide for making ethical decisions in conflict situations. Summarized the principle says that the responsible person must in all situations seek to maximize the good and true values present and to minimize the bad and the disvalues present. Or, as my colleague Father Timothy O'Connell says, one ought to do as much good as possible and as little evil as necessary.

Properly catechized Catholics, of course, know that one may *never* "do evil that good may come of it" (Rom 3:8). Father Place is simply using the NCD as a convenient vehicle to expound the new moral theology; in no way does the document reflect or even allow such an interpretation. Father Place went on:

> . . . so, too, personal sin then is not as easily identified with the doing of a particular "bad act." Personal sin comes about when one refuses to live the creation destiny of being a responsible and relational person. . . . Ultimately a human action has the personal significance of selfishness as it is expressive of this fundamental perspective.[54]

On the contrary, the NCD itself (no. 165) plainly recognizes that sin is personal and that "the choice of sin occurs in the human heart, and sin is expressed through personal choices and actions". In all these thoughts on controverted issues in moral theology, Father Place never found any place to mention that many respected moralists today strenuously and cogently oppose the moral approach he describes; his approach has been criticized as a form of consequentialism that requires the abandonment of moral absolutes and implies that the end justifies the means.

Not surprisingly, the bishops have not endorsed his point of view, either in the NCD or anywhere else; but neither *The Living*

[54] Ibid., pp. 167–84.

Light nor the USCC Department of Education sponsoring it, apparently, really feel they have to be tied down to what the bishops may have decided—or what the Catholic people proved they wanted in the course of the consultations for *Sharing the Light of Faith.*

8.

In November 1976, while the NCD consultation process was still in full swing, the National Conference of Catholic Bishops submitted a report to the General Secretariat of the Synod of Bishops for the Synod of 1977 that was scheduled to deal with the topic: "Catechetics in Our Time with Special Reference to Children and Young People". Data obtained from a questionnaire designed by the NCCB ad hoc Committee for the Synod represented responses from forty-nine dioceses and formed the basis of the report submitted to the Holy See in preparation for the Synod. Since this was the one occasion during the postconciliar period when the Church in the United States produced a general report on religious education, it may be helpful to outline a number of the findings in the report, supplementing the material covered in the present study. The official report covered what it identified as both positive and negative developments in the years after Vatican II.

The report indicated the general acceptance accorded to the introduction into catechesis of developments occurring in the specialized areas of Scripture, theology, patristics, liturgy, social doctrine, and ecumenism. Next in importance and level of approval was the integration into catechesis of findings in psychology, education, anthropology, and sociology.

The use of experience, everyday situations, occurrences and problems, in short, experiential learning, was cited by many as a valuable means for assuring that the content of catechesis would be more readily understandable, practical, and livable. The report itself observed: "The respondents saw this as the general acceptance of the inductive-experiential pedagogy as contrasted with deductive-abstract learning which has been emphasized over the past 500 years."[55]

Introduction into catechesis of developments in the ecclesiastical and human sciences, along with the employment of experiential learning, were said to have contributed significantly to the improvement of religious education methodologies, allowing them to develop from the informational to the adaptive, to the kerygmatic, and finally to the experiential emphasis approaches. (There is apparently no argument concerning the facts about how the modern catechetical movement developed; the argument comes when considering what these particular developments have meant and mean for Catholic religious education.) It was also indicated that music, art, drama, mime, literature, and apostolic activities had also been incorporated into the presentation of the message as a result of these contemporary methodologies. These vehicles of instruction were cited as producing a balance between the communication of content and the tapping of the emotional, intellectual, physical, and motivational potentialities of the recipient of catechesis.

Textbooks were said to have benefited from the introduction of the developments just mentioned. Movies, filmstrips, records, tapes, cassettes, videotapes, photos, posters, banners, and art prints were said to "have enlarged the possibilities for effective communication". The "professionalization" of catechists was considered next in order of importance and the report observed that the success of the catechetical program on the local level was directly related to the presence of "a fulltime professionally trained catechists with leadership abilities". The emergence of graduate schools of religious education, diocesan catechetical institutes, and other training modalities for teacher preparation was approvingly commented upon by contributors to the report.

The growing involvement of parents in the catechesis of their children, especially in preparation for the reception of the first

[55] National Conference of Catholic Bishops, "The State of Catechesis: Report to the Synod Secretariat", in *Origins,* NC Documentary Service, April 21, 1977.

sacraments, was applauded, and it was stated that programs involving parents in the overall catechetical enterprise had proven to be the most successful in this country.

Approval of the recognition, in principle, of adult religious education as "an integral and indeed prime form" of catechesis was mentioned by many dioceses despite the mixed results in the success of these programs. A fair number of respondents commented favorably upon a recent shift toward a more family-centered approach to catechesis and indicated that family religious education would be one of the major trends in the future.

The report discussed another significant trend, the growth of youth ministry that involves ministering to all the needs of the young person, including catechetical development. The effectiveness of "peer ministry", that is, ministry by temperamentally suited and properly trained persons who are about the same age as the youths being served, was discussed by a number of respondents.

Among other developments in catechesis that received some consideration in the report were the following: the realization that catechesis is a lifelong process; the recognition that faith is a free choice rather than ethnic or cultural identification; the efforts to apply contemporary knowledge regarding the stages of human development to moral growth; catechetical promotion of ecumenical awareness; and concern for the evaluation of teaching content, methods, and materials.

The report then considered developments during the previous twenty years that had hindered catechesis. An initial observation was that many serious problems had actually been noncatechetical in origin or motive. Chief among these had been the breakdown in the cultural order. Since the United States could be said to have been distancing itself from at least a semblance of allegiance to and practice of Christian values, moving to the status of a secularized and, in many respects, amoral society, the Catholic community had been significantly influenced by such a trend.

In the view of the report, "this impact has been heightened by the breakup of many Catholic neighborhoods and a movement to the suburbs". Changes in society, such as the deterioration of the family, mounting divorce rates, one-parent families, working mothers, the use of drugs, and abortion, were also seen to have had a serious impact on the Catholic community.

The dramatic increase of recreational and educational opportunities competing with religious activities—and especially with religious education—was also termed important by several respondents.

The "confusion, ambiguity, distrust, fear, and even hostility and anger produced by the changes that took place in the Church in the wake of the Second Vatican Council" were considered among the most serious handicaps to effective catechesis. The report went on to observe that while this was felt in all areas of Catholic life, religious education became one of the major battlegrounds for those who had opposing views on the Church and the world. Confusion often led to polarization and serious tensions between "progressives" and "conservatives". In several instances the situation led to crises of faith and to disaffiliation from the Church.

Many dioceses reported that among the aspects of polarization affecting catechesis had been the division that developed between theologians and the magisterium. This had resulted, in some cases, in the inability or failure of teachers to make a sufficiently clear distinction between matters of theological speculation and research and what is held and taught by the magisterium. It was noted that the process, in this regard, has filtered down from the level of university, seminary, and college to elementary- and secondary-level religious education programs.

Interestingly enough the report, in its concluding section, called for the establishment of dialogue between the hierarchy and scholars, particularly theologians:

> Often the conclusions of theologians and the teachings of bishops do not agree. Since the theologian, and not the bishop, is the real teacher of the catechist, the former sets the tone for what is being taught in catechesis at all levels, virtually throughout the country. This tension, if it is to be resolved, will require serious and extensive dialogue between theologians and bishops.

There appears to be no other way of dealing with this real and serious problem.[56]

Blame for the ensuing confusion and polarization was assigned to the inadequate implementation of Vatican II and the ineffective communication of developments in the catechetical field. Changes were not accompanied by opportunities for all concerned to understand, internalize, and participate in renewal. The NCCB report was quick to note, however, that this was equally true of parents and catechists as well as clergy and some religious.

Although some lauded modern catechetical textbooks, others criticized them, complaining that textbook series were "inaccurate, hurriedly written and foisted on the public" and lacked essential elements of doctrine and morality. This contributed to the anti-intellectual approach of the late sixties and early seventies, a period sometimes referred to as the age of "glorious uncertainty". This produced, in the opinion of some diocesan respondents to the report, nearly a whole generation "devoid of knowledge of the faith". Such an approach implicitly denied that the committed Catholic is a thinking, rational being as well as a "feeling, desiring person".

The existence of continued division regarding the cognitive versus the affective and the deductive versus inductive dimension of catechesis was also pointed out. Some maintained that cognitive and deductive approaches continued to dominate, so that religion was treated as a subject rather than a life to be lived, while others indicated that the affective and inductive approaches so dominated catechesis that psychological reactions rather than spiritual and intellectual growth were considered more important outcomes for the religious education enterprise. The abandonment of memorization as a legitimate pedagogical device was considered unfortunate by several respondents.

The tendency to substitute value clarification techniques for moral theology, to consider morality outside of a religious context and the Catholic tradition, and even to deny the objective norms of morality was strongly opposed by several respondents.

[56] Ibid.

A number of dioceses observed that there had been a tendency to follow fads and to use gimmicks, gadgets, and novelties in catechesis. Frequent switching from one religious education program to another with little or no continuity in scope were seen to have negative results. Some lamented the tendency to view every new development in the field as a final answer instead of but one further element in catechesis requiring serious evaluation.

The report indicated that the loss of credibility in the Church's mission, occasioned by the resignation of a significant number of priests and religious from their respective ministries and apostolates, had proven harmful to catechesis. Complaints were also registered about the lack of pastoral support and supervision, a frequent result of priests abdicating their positions as the ones ultimately responsible for religious education programs. The lack of professionally trained religious educators was also singled out as a negative element in the current field of religious education. Many had received neither theological nor pedagogical preparation to teach religion, a situation that impeded rather than encouraged faith development. Selection of teachers was often made on the basis of availability without sufficient regard for their qualifications. A few diocesan reports noted that some catechists lacked sensitivity and proper discretion in projecting their personal crises—such as those of vocation or faith—and thus they sometimes disturbed the young people or adults whom they were teaching.

A few other negative influences that were treated included the following: the failure to set up a national catechetical and pastoral institute to provide research and programs; the persistence of child-centered catechesis; and downgrading the importance of parochial schools, thereby depriving many children and youth of the opportunity of a sound, integrated religious formation.

One hopeful element mentioned frequently in the NCCB report was the process then going on for the preparation of the *National Catechetical Directory;* it was hoped that the issuance of this document would mark the beginning of the end of some of the perceived problems recounted in the report.

Thus did the National Conference of Catholic Bishops report

on the state of catechesis in the United States in preparation for the 1977 Synod of Bishops to be devoted to the subject of catechesis.

9.

The previous section provided a bare, unadorned summary of how the National Conference of Catholic Bishops officially saw the state of catechesis in the United States in the mid-seventies—roughly during the period of the developments in the catechetical movement leading to perceived deficiencies in religious education followed by the official efforts to correct the situation that have been chronicled in this and the previous chapter. Since this was the only time the Church in the United States ever officially assessed the teaching of religion in the postconciliar era, it was considered important to provide a summary of what the bishops included in their report. The developments recounted and discussed in the course of this study will be seen to be quite consistent with what the bishops themselves admitted in their official NCCB report to the Synod, although needless to say, several features such as doctrineless and experiential catechesis and an exaggerated kind of professionalization have been emphasized and highlighted in this study to a much greater extent than could be expected to be the case in a necessarily bland and impersonal official report.

Still, it is worth noting here too that many of the positive factors mentioned in the NCCB report are quite accurate, although they have not been particularly the focus of the present study. It is quite true that many, many Catholics have gone on teaching and learning the authentic faith of Christ throughout the entire period covered here; many, many Catholic religion teachers have never ceased, with the help of God, to understand and act on the obvious truth that the point of Catholic catechesis is to hand on the authentic faith of Jesus Christ as expounded by the magisterium of the Church; such teachers have been as baffled as pastors and parents by a catechesis that apparently downgrades, distorts, or omits important features of Catholic teaching in the name of whatever new thing appears on the horizon.

There have been, indeed, in the course of the postconciliar period, many expressions of what may be considered a veritable hunger for the authentic faith. For example, two outstanding adult catechisms were published during the general period being covered here, and both became runaway best sellers: they were *The Catholic Catechism,* by Father John A. Hardon, S.J., published in 1975[57], and *The Teaching of Christ,* by Ronald Lawler, O.F.M. Cap., Donald W. Wuerl (now bishop of Pittsburgh, who would also be on Rome's panel of "experts" for the Catechism for the Universal Church), and Thomas Comerford Lawler, written with fourteen other co-authors and published in 1976.[58]

Similarly much later, in 1990, Ignatius Press published a translation of a German catechism for adults that had quickly sold a quarter of a million copies in the first year of its publication in Germany: *The Church's Confession of Faith.*[59] This adult catechism was a book on which both Cardinal Ratzinger and the well-known German theologian Walter Kasper, now bishop of Stuttgart-Rottenburg, had worked; this book also testifies to the existence of a veritable hunger for the authentic Catholic faith. In response to this hunger many diocesan and parish directors of religious education and many, many catechists have gone right on teaching the faith regardless of what the NCDDRE or the USCC Department of Education may have been doing.

Nevertheless, not even the official NCCB report denied the existence of the kinds of catechetical deficiencies identified in this study in connection with developments in catechesis followed by the reactions to the Church's issuance of the *General Catechetical Directory* and the U.S. bishops' *Basic Teachings for Catholic Religious Education.* These deficiencies followed a fundamental "crisis

[57] John A. Hardon, S.J., *The Catholic Catechism* (Garden City, N.Y.: Doubleday, 1975).

[58] Ronald Lawler, O.F.M. Cap., Donald W. Wuerl, and Thomas Comerford Lawler, eds. *The Teaching of Christ: A Catholic Catechism for Adults* (Huntington, Ind.: Our Sunday Visitor, 1976).

[59] German Conference of Catholic Bishops, *The Church's Confession of Faith: A Catholic Catechism for Adults* (San Francisco: Ignatius Press, 1990).

of faith" identified by Pope Paul VI at the time of the Dutch Catechism affair; and, on the evidence presented in this study, this crisis of faith surely remains the most important single factor in the state of catechesis in the United States even up to the present day. This is also true elsewhere than in the United States, of course. It is no exaggeration to say that every major effort of the hierarchy to try to remedy the perceived defects in current catechesis and to insure that the faith was being handed on in its fullness has been undermined in one way or another by the official catechetical establishment—by the very people who, under the bishops, were most responsible for handing on the faith. In the post-conciliar era the new theologians and their disciples in the catechetical movement have clearly had another agenda than the one consistently laid down by the hierarchy.

The present study began with a review of the reception given by *The Universal Catechism Reader* people to Rome's draft Catechism for the Universal Church. It quickly became clear that this group of Catholic scholars had another and different agenda than the Church's; the evidence leaped to the eye. Now it is clear that there was nothing new or original in this group's assault on official (and authentic) Roman Catholicism as embodied in both the process and the product of the Catechism: the same thing has been going on virtually since the end of the Second Vatican Council. The only thing different about this most recent effort is that the undermining of the official Church document being aimed at began before the document in question could even be completed and issued—this is probably a measure of the importance of the document.

In view of the sad reality of disloyalty to authentic Church teaching and direction that has been documented and discussed especially in the present chapter, it might be asked why the bishops continued to rely on people to carry out the task of religious education who were so quickly and consistently able and willing to undermine the very official efforts being exerted to return soundness to catechesis and insure that what was taught in Catholic schools and religious education programs was indeed the

Catholic faith. Why did there never seem to be much of a negative reaction from the hierarchy whenever its latest effort turned out to have been, once again, undermined by the very religious education establishment commissioned to carry it out? Why were educators such as Fathers Thomas Sullivan and Berard Marthaler not removed from positions of influence in catechesis when their unwillingness to follow the Church had become so clear? Why was there never any attempt on the part of the bishops to follow up to see if the *Basic Teachings,* for example, *were* in fact being "stressed in the religious formation of Catholics of all ages"?

There is probably no simple answer to these questions. Catholic bishops today tend to be overscheduled and hard-pressed "managers". In the period under consideration they were frequently harassed men, trying to do a job with a steadily shrinking cadre of those who had traditionally been their principal assistants and collaborators, namely, priests and religious. This remains largely the case today.

But the professional religious educators generally tended to be priests and religious who had remained in place and were still seemingly able and willing to go on carrying out a task that the Church badly needed done. They presented themselves as loyal; the fiction always was that their aberrations were completely legitimate modern developments. Certainly the religious educators were rarely in an openly belligerent position actively "fighting" the bishops, as those protesting about the errors, distortions, or omissions in catechesis always seemed to be actively "fighting" the Church. Also, the religious educators were "inside" the system and could therefore easily appear to be doing the will of the bishops (although the frankness with which they sometimes disclaimed this in some of the documents they themselves produced was more than once little short of amazing—but then maybe the bishops were not reading NCDDRE or USCC documents). However that may be, the religious educators were never in a position of standing outside and vainly beating on the door with their protests, as those who were calling for sound catechesis so often seemed to be.

Moreover, the religious educators never failed to emphasize on every important occasion their own competence and professionalism in carrying out the task of catechesis confided to them, and they had their diplomas and degrees to prove it. Anyone still in possession of his integral Catholic faith such as, for instance, a bishop, probably had a difficult time imagining or visualizing how the catechetical movement could ever have given up the substance of the faith as easily as the catechetical movement demonstrably did, while going on to pursue utterly superficial fads and fashions. For this reason in particular bishops generally tended to believe reassurances that all was well when they were offered. Moreover, it was only too easy to believe also that the ones doing the complaining about catechesis, like those complaining about the new liturgy, were simply nostalgic for the pre–Vatican II Church, as well as being uncharitable, right wing, and so on; also, if this was accepted, it meant no one had to do anything about the complaints being made.

Another thing the religious educators were almost always able to do quite well was to lead the bishops away from familiar areas that the latter knew, such as theology and the faith, and lead them into the thickets of the new pedagogy, the new psychology, the new educational techniques, and so on, where the only possible guides the bishops had were the religious educators themselves. All in all, the whole situation was one with which, with the best will in the world, any hierarchy would have a hard time coping.

It might be asked too why the new religious educators themselves persisted so tenaciously in defending and diffusing their variant versions of Catholicism when they must have known when they were going contrary to what the Church required and enjoined. Can they ever have seriously imagined that a Pope John Paul II or a Cardinal Ratzinger, or even more than a handful of the U.S. bishops, would ever come actually to accept their new catechesis, once its true character had been brought out into the open? These questions too are probably ultimately unanswerable, but probable answers may grant that they certainly were aware that the present leadership in the Church would never accept their viewpoint. However, the new catechists have apparently been looking to the future and to the hope of new leadership more congenial to their views. It certainly is remarkable how long they have been tolerated and allowed the freedom of the Church; it has been only too easy for the unperceptive to imagine that with a more liberal pope or a few more bishops congenial to their views the whole thing could conceivably go their way. People in this frame of mind, for example, consider the election of a "conservative" pope from a communist country to have been a real fluke not likely to be repeated at the next conclave. The fact appears to be that they did and do hope to be able to take over the Church in the name of their own aberrant views, just as past heretics and schismatics in history have nourished the same kind of hope; for this reason they believe strongly in what they are doing and actively pursue and promote it. They have plenty of zeal, although as Saint Paul put it, "their zeal is unenlightened" (Rom 10:2). For no serious historian of the Church or the papacy is likely to grant them any odds on their hopes of changing the Church's view of her faith at some time in the future; but then for them too hope consists of things not seen.

All of these things were part of "the state of catechesis" wher the 1977 Synod of Bishops reviewed the whole subject. It was a subject that did not cease to trouble the hierarchy, for in spite of all of the latter's efforts, on one level at least, catechesis continued to be understood as a "bad scene". Since all of the efforts to date to remedy the situation seemed not to have remedied the situation, the road was fast opening up that would lead to the proposal at the 1985 Synod for a Catechism for the Universal Church.

Meanwhile though, the 1977 Synod had to take the next logical step; this was Pope John Paul II's apostolic exhortation *Catechesi Tradendae* on Catechesis in Our Time, which came out in October 1979. Reference has been made so frequently to this document in these pages that it need not be summarized in any detail. It is a short, readable, and easily available document that, if it had been or were to begin to be followed in its integrity, would by itself provide the needed remedy for what ails religious education today. It is worth noting, for example, how effortlessly John Paul II has integrated the best insights of the kerygmatic movement into the Church's own understanding of what is involved in catechesis:

> The Church has always considered catechesis one of her primary tasks, for, before Christ ascended to His Father after His resurrection, He gave the apostles a final command—to make disciples of all nations and to teach them to observe all that He had commanded. He thus entrusted them with the mission and power to proclaim to humanity what they had heard, what they had seen with their eyes, what they had looked upon and touched with their hands, concerning the Word of Life. He also entrusted them with the mission and power to explain with authority what He had taught them, His words and actions, His signs and commandments. And He gave them the Spirit to fulfill this mission.[60]

Here we certainly do have experiential catechesis—but it has reference to the experience of the apostles. *Catechesi Tradendae* was also not afraid to emphasize what had proved enduringly effective in the Church's long tradition of catechesis, for example, memorization:

> The final methodological question the importance of which should at least be referred to—one that was debated several times in the Synod—is that of memorization. In the beginnings of Christian catechesis, which co-incided with a civilization that was mainly oral, recourse was had very freely to memorization. Catechesis has since then known a long tradition of learning the principal truths by memorizing. We are all aware that this method can present certain disadvantages, not the least of which is that it lends itself to insufficient or at times almost non-existent assimilation, reducing all knowledge to formulas that are repeated without being properly understood. These disadvantages and the different characteristics of our own civilization have in some places led to the almost complete suppression—according to some, alas, the definitive suppression—of memori-

[60] John Paul II, *Catechesi Tradendae,* no. 25.

zation in catechesis. And yet certain very authoritative voices made themselves heard on the occasion of the fourth general assembly of the Synod, calling for restoration of a judicious balance between reflection and spontaneity, between dialogue and silence, between written work and memory work. Moreover certain cultures still set great value on memorization.[61]

On this subject of memorization John Paul II concluded with an expression not easily forgotten: "Faith and piety", he declared, "do not grow in the desert places of a memory-less catechesis."[62] Nor, it might be added to conclude this chapter, do they grow out of a creedless, doctrineless catechesis unwilling to be subject to the authority and direction of the Church and the efforts of her sacred hierarchy to establish what catechesis has to be if it is to be faithful to the commission of Christ to the apostles.

[61] Ibid., no. 55.
[62] Ibid.

Chapter IV

Conclusion

I.

The present study has followed a rather long and occasionally circuitous route up to this point, but it is quite clear from what has been covered that the 1985 Synod of Bishops' proposal for a Catechism for the Universal Church was an inevitable development in the history of the post–Vatican II Church. It was equally inevitable that the Holy See would accept the Synod's proposal and set vigorously to work on the project with Rome's customary tenacity and resolve. Those familiar with the long history of the Holy See know that usually only temporarily can this See be turned aside from its appointed task. A Churchwide catechism—a clear and comprehensive statement of the Church's faith for teaching purposes and as a "point of reference"—has proved to be a practical necessity a quarter of a century after the Council.

The twenty-plus year period after the Council during which a "directory" was supposed to be the guide for the Church's transmission of her faith by means of formal catechesis has turned out to be a most unrepresentative period in the history of the Church over the past half millenium and more. This is not because there was anything wrong with the *General Catechetical Directory,* or indeed, with the U.S. *National Catechetical Directory, Sharing the Light of Faith,* which derived from the GCD and represented a truly honest effort by the Church in the United States. On the contrary, as was brought out in Chapter 3, both of these documents turned out to be sound and useful documents, quite responsive to the hopes of their sponsors.

The trouble was, though, as has now been abundantly shown in the course of this study, a large, influential, and entrenched body of "emancipated", "professional" religious educators showed themselves determined not to follow the direction of the Church in catechesis, whether as expressed in the GCD or the NCD, or in any of the other documents such as Pope John Paul II's *Catechesi Tradendae* that the Church has from time to time seen fit to issue insisting on the integrity and authenticity of her traditional faith, regardless of what some moderns may have come to think about it, and demanding that it be handed on in a manner consonant with the Church's own "living, active *tradition*", as Pope John Paul II has expressed it.[1] "Tradition" *means* something delivered or handed down, not something dreamed up to fit the supposed needs or requirements of the moment.

In the present study all this has been shown mostly in relation to the American scene, or to the impact of Roman words and acts on the American scene, with the important exception of the Dutch Catechism. It could equally have been shown, however, with reference to developments in catechesis in other countries, especially European countries, in the postconciliar years, for the problems covered in this study have been rather widespread in the Church generally. A recent article on the catechetical situation in France, for example, reveals the existence of a similar creedless, doctrineless, noncognitive kind of catechesis being promoted by the catechetical establishment there. In France the religious educators appear determined to bypass Rome certainly, and their own bishops if necessary, in promoting their own agenda of what appears to be a new Christianity and a new Catholicism, as imagined by them.

In the early eighties a new approach to catechesis was mounted in France. It included as a basic document something called *Pierres Vivantes* ("Living Stones"), which was a collection of reference texts of documents related to the faith; these texts were divided into three sections: "the Book of the Covenant", "Christians in History", and "Celebrations and Prayers". There were included

[1] Pope John Paul II, Apostolic Exhortation *Catechesi Tradendae* on Catechesis in Our Time, October 16, 1979, no. 22.

among these basic texts many references from both the Old and the New Testaments. However, the presentation did not follow the usual chronological order of salvation history, from creation to redemption by Christ. Rather, it told the story in more generic terms and also summarized Church history, highlighting "great events", including the Second Vatican Council.

These basic texts were designed to be supplemented in each diocese by what were called *parcours catéchétiques* ("catechetical journeys"), adapted to a given sociocultural context. A number of these *parcours* were prepared and approved by the French Episcopal Commission for Religious Education. The stated intentions of the creators of *Pierres Vivantes* and the French bishops who sponsored it was to produce the best possible updated catechism; no doubt these intentions were of the best.

Two things occurred in rapid succession, however, that were unfortunately all too typical of postconciliar catechesis generally: (1) In 1982, French dioceses officially adopted *Pierres Vivantes* and proscribed all other texts then in use; and (2) the texts, and indeed the whole approach, simultaneously became the subjects of various protests about the way the faith was being taught:

> As soon as they appeared, the new texts met with vehement criticism both in France and abroad. *Pierres Vivantes* was accused of being vague to the point of reticence on truths that are central to the faith such as original sin, the soul, and Christ's ascension. In addition, its shift of focus from the objectivity of facts to the "conscience" of the disciples and their community induces subjectivity, reducing the Christian fact to a mere "story". According to the critics, the defects and deviations were more serious still in the *parcours,* accused of blatant liberalism and of giving a sociological and symbolical interpretation to central tenets of the Christian faith. . . . [2]

All this, of course, reads depressingly like a reportage from the American scene as covered in the present study. Bishop Emile

[2] Gianni Valente, "The Text of Contention: *Pierres Vivantes*", in *Thirty Days,* January 1991.

Marcus of Nantes was obliged to declare in April 1983 that the whole experiment had "fallen short of its essential objective: to provide a clear affirmation of faith".[3]

It was in the midst of this situation that Cardinal Joseph Ratzinger visited France and delivered two memorable lectures in Paris and Lyons, in the course of which he made the statement, already quoted in this study, that "the suppression of the catechism and the declaration that its format was out of date" was "a serious error".[4] This statement by the prefect of the Congregation for the Doctrine of the Faith was surely one of the most important of all the antecedents of Cardinal Bernard Law's proposal to the 1985 Synod of Bishops that a Catechism for the Universal Church be prepared and promulgated.

In France there followed the now familiar process of consultations between Rome and the French conference of bishops on the subject of *Pierres Vivantes.* Revisions were ordered, and some were made. Predictably, "French catechists did not welcome Rome's intervention. Some talked of interference, while others doubted the legitimacy of Rome's action as far as 'ordinary' catechetical affairs are concerned."[5]

All this should be very familiar by now, and yet it still might not be familiar enough to prevent anyone trying to call attention to it from being labeled "right wing", "extremist", "reactionary", "preconciliar", or something of the sort. These epithets applied to those who do not accept the new catechesis have been all too effectively applied in the postconciliar era by those who think that their particular interpretations of "the signs of the times" should somehow supersede the faith handed down in the Church. The satisfaction of knowing oneself to be in harmony with the true

[3] Ibid.

[4] Ibid. See also Cardinal Joseph Ratzinger, "Sources and Transmission of the Faith", *Communio* 10 (1983): 18, quoted by Berard L. Marthaler, OFM Conv., "Catechetical Directory or Catechism: *Une Question Mal Posée*", in Dermot A. Lane, ed., *Religious Education and the Future* (Dublin, Ireland: Columba Press, 1986).

[5] Ibid.

mind of the Church, however, will generally compensate quite adequately for whatever one may come to be called for espousing and defending the true faith.

2.

The Catechism for the Universal Church will be issued in 1992, or perhaps somewhat later, and thereafter will be *the* "point of reference" for the teaching of religion in the Catholic Church. By this is meant simply that in case of questions or doubts, the Catechism will be the work that will necessarily have to be referred to for a resolution of these questions or doubts; the Catechism will be the place where "the buck stops", to employ a more American idiom. Thus, it is impossible to exaggerate the importance of this Catechism, as both friends and foes of the project have understood; it is so important that what came to be the habitual postconciliar process of undermining this kind of document and trying to bring it into disrepute has begun even before the issuance of the document itself.

The present study has not aimed at looking at the draft Catechism or at providing a critique of its text or suggestions for improvement. The present writer participated in the consultation process in my capacity as Special Consultant for Religious Education to my ordinary, Cardinal John O'Connor. This study, however, as explained at the outset, has aimed at trying to explain the context and environment out of which the Catechism came and into which it will go. The time has now come to conclude this whole study, and to do so, several brief recommendations are offered:

1. The Catechism for the Universal Church can be relied on when promulgated. The Holy See is the guarantor of its authenticity. Ample consultation with the bishops of the world has been afforded and has been taken advantage of; both the process and the product are worthy of confidence. As has been verified in this study, Rome's record for issuing documents and instructions that are right on the mark is little short of uncanny from a purely

empirical standpoint and should give real pause to those who go on talking as if Roman documents represented just another "theology". This position, in fact, is inconsistent with affirming the Catholic faith itself in its fullness. Therefore the time has come for a permanent moratorium on criticizing and undermining the documents of the Holy See as if they were just one more subject for debate, scholarly or otherwise. The faith has hardly been helped by all the sniping and carping, the refusal to accept as valid what those who have the commission from Christ to do have legitimately ordained. Catholics have a right to their faith unblurred by being viewed through whatever scholarly, ideological, or polemical lenses. Those who find that they cannot accept the Catechism from the hands of the legitimate authority of the Church should, in all honesty, move into some other line of work or endeavor.

2. When the Catechism for the Universal Church is promulgated, the Holy See should establish in Rome a permanent Pontifical Commission for the Authentic Interpretation of the Catechism for the Universal Church. This can be done on the model of the Pontifical Commission for the Authentic Interpretation of Canon Law, which succeeded the Commission on the Revision of Canon Law once the latter had completed its almost twenty-year-long task of revising the Code of Canon Law with the issuance of the new Code in 1983. This Roman Commission should be empowered to decide, in the case of disputed questions, which national, regional, or local catechisms are, in whole or in part, in conformity with the Catechism for the Universal Church. Bishops' conferences as well as individual dioceses should establish similar commissions for the Catechism—*not,* by the way, composed only of catechetical experts; the record of the postconciliar religious education establishment is, unfortunately, clear enough by now so that these people should no longer be allowed to go on being the advocates, judges, and juries in their own cases, as has too often been the situation in the postconciliar era to date.

3. The Holy See, bishops' conferences, and individual dioceses should sponsor, either under the auspices of the commissions

proposed above or under other appropriate auspices, intensive and extensive courses, conferences, lectures, lessons, studies, booklets, institutes, and the like on the subject of the Catechism for the Universal Church. Once again, these should *not* be barely concealed exercises in explaining away or otherwise undermining the Catechism conducted by partisans of the new catechesis, as has too often been the case in the postconciliar era. Hence the bishops themselves should maintain direct and immediate control over these activities, monitoring them closely and allowing only those prepared to accept the new Catechism wholeheartedly to participate. If the catechetical movement could achieve the far-reaching effects that it did through a half dozen International Catechetical Study Weeks in Eichstätt, Bangkok, Manila, and so on, there is certainly no reason why the Church should not be able to mount a valid countermovement with the help of that vast majority in the Church called the Catholic faithful, those who love and are desirous of the authentic Catholic faith.

4. The training of religion teachers must be carried out entirely in accordance with the principles of the new Catechism for the Universal Church as soon as the latter is promulgated. Indeed it is not too soon to begin working on this activity now. It will not serve to promulgate the Catechism only to allow those who will be responsible for implementing it to go right on being trained in courses and institutes conducted by new theologians and new religion teachers who are dissenters and have a different agenda from the Church's agenda. The appearance of *The Universal Catechism Reader,* by the way, should serve as fair warning to the Church in the United States about what will surely be *attempted* in the way of undermining and discrediting the Catechism. It has already begun in fact, and so there is no excuse for not remembering that there is a determined group of people out there who have been laying for this Catechism since it was first conceived back in 1985, and who have vowed that it will not be "received" by the Catholic people if they have anything to say about it.

5. Not only schools of education and catechetical institutes must be required to be in conformity with the Catechism for the

Universal Church; the catechisms and textbooks that are actually published and put into the hands of students must also be in conformity. Religion textbook publishers over the past quarter of a century have tended to look not to the direct enactments of the Church in this regard but rather to their friends and contacts in the catechetical movement and the religious education establishment. Thus, with rare exceptions, the *General Catechetical Directory,* the *Basic Teachings,* the *National Catechetical Directory,* and *Catechesi Tradendae* were never required, in any systematic way with follow-up included, to be incorporated into the actual religion texts and religious education materials being published. There is a yawning gap here that henceforth has to be filled. The good will of the professional catechetical people cannot be depended upon to see that this is done; the actual record points in a contrary direction. The hierarchy promulgated excellent doctrinal and methodological guidance with consistency, but there was generally little follow-up, and what the hierarchy laid down was often not picked up and incorporated into the actual books and materials in use. This same situation must not be repeated in the case of the Catechism for the Universal Church; the Catholic people have a right to their faith, whole and entire and unadulterated, and self-appointed and self-interested groups who think they know better do not have the right to try to deprive the Catholic people of this authentic faith. One hopeful sign in this regard, although it was only a beginning, was the "Guidelines for Doctrinally Sound Catechetical Materials" adopted by the U.S. bishops at their annual fall meeting in November 1990.[6] It is simply amazing, considering the controversies that have raged over the teaching of religion virtually since the Council and the subsequent emergence of the new catechesis that the hierarchy never, until 1990, attempted to lay down any actual requirements for religion textbook publishers. But their good intentions in this regard have now been

[6] National Conference of Catholic Bishops, "Guidelines for Doctrinally Sound Catechetical Materials", in *Origins,* CNS Documentary Service, December 13, 1990.

announced; it is a course upon which they have now embarked and must diligently pursue.

6. There are fine priests and religious educators out there who want the faith and are loyal to the Church, and who will faithfully implement the new Catechism; the bishops should seek them out and make use of them, and not allow themselves to make their judgments concerning religion teaching on the basis of what is said to be up to date, "the state of the art", or the latest thing; it is time to go back to the original, authentic, and real thing.

In a word, the Catechism for the Universal Church must represent an entirely new era when the faith will again be seen and recognized by all as "the Catholic faith that comes to us from the apostles" (First Eucharistic Prayer).

Abbreviations

CCD	Confraternity of Christian Doctrine
CDF	Congregation for the Doctrine of the Faith
DRE	Director of Religious Education
FCS	Fellowship of Catholic Scholars
GCD	*General Catechetical Directory*
NCCB	National Conference of Catholic Bishops
NCD	*National Catechetical Directory*
NCDDRE	National Conference of Diocesan Directors of Religious Education
NCEA	National Catholic Education Association
RCIA	Rite of Christian Initiation for Adults
REOI	Religious Education Outcomes Inventory
USCC	U. S. Catholic Conference

Index